"*Daniel Rudd: Calling a Church to Justice* is an engaging introduction for those who have never heard of Daniel Rudd and a fascinating study for those who already know a good deal about the man and his mission. Using Daniel Rudd's newspaper, *The American Catholic Tribune,* as his primary source, Gary Agee allows readers to hear in Rudd's own words why he was committed both to the Catholic Church and the African American community, and learn how Rudd came to his absolute conviction that Catholicism truly lived, understood, and applied was the best chance for justice for people of African descent in the United States. Daniel Rudd is one of the most intriguing and inspiring U.S. Catholics of the 19th century. Agee's book helps us to see why this is so."

   —Cecilia A. Moore
    University of Dayton

"Black Catholicism is personified in the life and legacy of Daniel Rudd. Gary Agee masterfully chronicles the successes and struggles, the opportunities and obstacles that Rudd encountered as he made his mark on both the Church and society as newspaper publisher, founder of the Black Catholic Congress movement and advocate for racial justice. Present-day Black Catholics are forever indebted to the nascent visionary actions of Daniel Rudd."

   —Rev. Maurice J. Nutt, CSsR, DMin
    Director, Institute for Black Catholic Studies
    Xavier University of Louisiana

People of God

Remarkable Lives, Heroes of Faith

People of God is a series of inspiring biographies for the general reader. Each volume offers a compelling and honest narrative of the life of an important twentieth- or twenty-first-century Catholic. Some living and some now deceased, each of these women and men has known challenges and weaknesses familiar to most of us but responded to them in ways that call us to our own forms of heroism. Each offers a credible and concrete witness of faith, hope, and love to people of our own day.

John XXIII	Massimo Faggioli
Oscar Romero	Kevin Clarke
Thomas Merton	Michael W. Higgins
Francis	Michael Collins
Flannery O'Connor	Angela O'Donnell
Martin Sheen	Rose Pacatte
Jean Vanier	Michael W. Higgins
Dorothy Day	Patrick Jordan
Luis Antonio Tagle	Cindy Wooden
Georges and Pauline Vanier	Mary Francis Coady
Joseph Bernardin	Steven P. Millies
Corita Kent	Rose Pacatte
Daniel Rudd	Gary B. Agee
Helen Prejean	Joyce Duriga
Paul VI	Michael Collins
Thea Bowman	Maurice J. Nutt
Shahbaz Bhatti	John L. Allen Jr.
Rutilio Grande	Rhina Guidos

More titles to follow. . . .

Daniel Rudd

Calling a Church to Justice

Gary B. Agee

LITURGICAL PRESS
Collegeville, Minnesota
www.litpress.org

Cover design by Red+Company. Cover illustration by Philip Bannister.

1   2   3   4   5   6   7   8   9

Library of Congress Control Number: 2016955868

ISBN 978-0-8146-4525-3   978-0-8146-4698-4 (ebook)

Contents

Acknowledgments

Many thanks to my wife and children, who paint the world in shades of green and blue, and to my beloved congregations who support me in the pursuit of this vocation. A special thanks to the University of Arkansas Press for its generosity in allowing me to rework portions of a previous biography of Daniel Rudd, *A Cry For Justice, Daniel Rudd and his Life in Black Catholicism, Journalism and Activism, 1854–1933* (2011). Credit should be extended to Liturgical Press for recognizing the importance of Rudd's life and work and to Barry Hudock for getting this project off the ground. Finally, I extend gratitude to Cecilia Moore who introduced me to Rudd, and to my colleague and friend, William L. Portier, who encouraged me in the writing of my dissertation on the subject of this book.

Introduction

In May of 1890, *The Christian Soldier*, an African American newspaper published from Lexington, Kentucky, declared "Dan A. Rudd of the Catholic Tribune" to be "the greatest negro Catholic in America."[1] If you do not know the name Daniel Arthur Rudd, you will find yourself in the company of many Catholics who have yet to discover this visionary's important contribution to the Catholic Church and to the cause of social justice in the United States. Over the past few years, however, more and more attention has been paid to Rudd as the church has become increasingly aware of the contributions of the persons making up the rich diversity within her. It is to the credit of historians including David Spalding, CFX; Cyprian Davis, OSB; and Joseph Lackner, SM; that Rudd's life and work have been uncovered for succeeding generations to consider.

I first became acquainted with Daniel Rudd while working to complete a reading course on black Catholics in the United States. Having an interest in the scourge of racism infecting the American church, I found Rudd's critique of the country's drift toward Jim Crow and racial segregation compelling. His insistence that the Catholic Church would play a leading role in the recognition of the full equality of African Americans was unique among black journalists of

1

his era. Rudd promoted this church-centered program of justice in his weekly newspaper, the *American Catholic Tribune*, published from 1886–1897. Because of my interest in Rudd's life and work, his understanding of justice became the subject of my PhD dissertation completed at the University of Dayton in 2008. This present biography is the fruit of that research.

It is fitting that the "People of God" series of biographies honoring important twentieth- and twenty-first-century Catholics would make room for a volume on Rudd; he is deserving of such attention. His success as a newspaper proprietor places him among the most able black journalists of his day. At the height of its popularity in 1892, as many as ten thousand copies of the *American Catholic Tribune* (*ACT*) were being distributed across the Midwest and eastern United States. In fact, Rudd's newspaper seems to have been so successful that in 1893 he would be called on to serve as president of the Afro-American Press Association,[2] an organization made up of the proprietors of the two hundred or so black newspapers being published at that time.

Also important to Rudd's legacy were his visionary efforts to bring Catholics together in order to address the challenges facing African Americans both in the church and in society. To this end, he worked to establish the Colored Catholic Congress movement that held its first gathering in Washington, DC, in 1889. The movement would go on to hold five congresses in the nineteenth century. This organization was established to aid members of the Catholic clergy (overwhelmingly white) in their efforts to evangelize African Americans. A bold and sometimes more controversial aspect of the work of the congress was to address the grievances of black Catholics, including those occasioned by instances of racial discrimination within the Catholic Church. This more contentious aspect of the work sometimes brought the congress movement into conflict with church leaders. Evidence from the *ACT* also seems to show Rudd may have been the primary instigator behind the formation of the Congress of Lay Catholics movement, an interracial initiative that sought to harness the gifts and talents of the laity for use in the work of the Catholic Church in the United States. In honor of the centennial of the establishment of the American church, the first meeting of the Congress of Lay Catholics was held in Baltimore in November 1889.

As a result of his work, Rudd won the confidence and praise of many important Catholic Church leaders both within the United States and abroad. Some of these individuals include Cardinal James Gibbons, archbishop of Baltimore; Cardinal Henry Edward Manning of Westminster, England; and Cardinal Charles Lavigerie, archbishop of Carthage and Algiers and primate of Africa. This is not to say that Rudd did not have his critics. For example, Joseph R. Slattery, the head of the American Josephites and the unofficial leader of the African American apostolate in the United States, worked at times to undermine Rudd's ministry, demonstrating that he had little confidence in the editor. Yet after extensive study, it appears this lack of confidence may have owed more to a streak of paternalism in Slattery than to any real deficiency in Rudd.[3]

Throughout Rudd's ministry he retained a positive view of the Catholic Church. In his editorials and speeches he communicated a persevering hope that the church would live up to its egalitarian ideals. Even when this divine institution denied educational opportunities to black students or was slow to ordain African American priests, Rudd remained faithful, placing the blame for the racial prejudice he encountered among his coreligionists on wayward individuals within the flock rather than on the official doctrine of his beloved church.

Rudd's confidence in the Catholic Church showed itself in his efforts to evangelize African Americans. His newspaper, the *ACT,* was published to recommend the Catholic faith to black Americans, the vast majority of whom attended Protestant churches during the period. But Rudd's faithfulness to Catholicism did not get in the way of his close collaboration with religious leaders of other denominational groups. In this regard he was a man ahead of his time. When there was a perceived injustice that called for redress, for example the lynching of a member of the black community, Rudd could be found among his Protestant brothers and sisters, standing shoulder to shoulder, adding his voice to a chorus protesting the injustice.

Though a study of Rudd's life and work is a worthy project, such an undertaking must not lead one to believe Rudd was the only noteworthy, nonwhite Catholic of his generation. A critical study of Christian history reminds us of the fact that individuals from nondominant groups, persons of color, women, and those whose earnings place them in the lowest economic income strata, have sometimes been slighted by historians. Daniel Rudd was part of a larger, active, albeit sometimes overlooked, black Catholic community.

Some other notable black Catholics making up this community include Bishop James Augustine Healy, the second bishop of Portland, Maine, and the first of African American heritage in the United States; Father Augustus Tolton, the first openly recognized priest of African American descent; Mother Mary Elizabeth Lange, who founded the country's first black religious order, the Oblate Sisters of Providence; and Mother Mathilda Taylor Beasley who founded the Third Order of St. Francis, a group of African American sisters, a school for black children, and subsequently an orphanage. More recent gifts to the church include, among others, Sister Beatrice Jefferies, vice president of the Sisters of the Blessed Sacrament, and Sister Thea Bowman of the Franciscan Sisters of Perpetual Adoration.

During the years Rudd published the *ACT*, he claimed there were not less than 200,000 black Catholics living in the United States. When individuals calculated a lesser figure, the editor pushed back. Rudd fought hard to defend his estimate because he wanted his readers, black and white, to realize African Americans were not an insignificant portion of the US Catholic population. Moreover, he wanted to make the case that large numbers of black seekers were moving into the church.

As with other Catholics of color, Rudd has been sometimes overlooked by historians. Though Cincinnati was the geographic center for much of Rudd's work, he is not even mentioned in John H. Lamott's *History of the Archdiocese of Cincinnati, 1821–1921*.[4] One is left with the question "why?" Because a key theme traced throughout the work is the spread of Catholicism throughout the region, Rudd's evangelistic work among African Americans would seem a fitting bit of history to include. Perhaps Lamott did not know Rudd or his work. Or maybe the omission can be explained by the distance between blacks and whites within the church in the first decades of the twentieth century. On the other hand, it may be that the author simply did not think his white readers would have an interest in the African American apostolate.

A focus on Rudd and his promotion of justice is not simply a matter of learning history—Rudd's dogged pursuit of justice seems relevant to the challenges facing twenty-first century society's most vulnerable individuals, including people of color. Topics addressed 130 years ago in the *ACT* appear in today's news cycle with disturbing regularity. Among these are racial and ethnic discrimination, voter access, fair wages, safe affordable housing, immigration policy, economic opportunity, and gender discrimination.

Rudd's concern for the evangelization of people of color at the end of the nineteenth century also rings true to similar efforts being promoted by church leaders today. As a part of the New Evangelization initiative encouraged by Pope Benedict XVI, the US Catholic bishops have initiated a program meant to provide a welcome atmosphere to the broad spectrum of diverse peoples entering Catholic churches around the country. At a recent training event funded by the United States Conference of Catholic Bishops (USCCB)—an event designed for trainers being equipped to promote intercultural competencies in parishes—I stumbled across a framed photo of Daniel Rudd prominently displayed in the session classroom. The presenter explained she was using the photo to illustrate the diversity within the Catholic Church.

The editor of the *ACT* trumpeted a similar message. He imagined the Catholic Church to be a universal body—one seeking to make room within her sanctuary for all races of people. Even as the nation moved headlong toward Jim Crow segregation, Rudd raised his voice in opposition to the discrimination being witnessed in the surrounding culture. He declared what he believed to be the foundational teaching of the church: the "Fatherhood of God and Brotherhood of Man." Familiar with Rudd's campaign for racial justice, it was encouraging to see a section on racism had been included in the USCCB training manual titled *Building Intercultural Competence for Ministers*. The kind of advocacy for justice and racial equality mirrors the work Rudd believed the church might take up in his own day. The editor of the *ACT*'s hopeful spirit attends the efforts of contemporary church leaders.

Telling the story of Daniel Rudd presents a number of challenges. For unlike other subjects in this "People of God" series whose biographical wanderings are easy to trace, Rudd's are not. He left for posterity no journal or collection of biographical notes. Having no heirs to fill in gaps in what we don't know of his life and work, we are sometimes left to speculate. But what Rudd *did* leave us are his letters, transcribed speeches, and more importantly his newspaper editorials. These we find printed in the extant issues of the *ACT*. At times his words are instructive, sometimes inspiring, and even challenging. They are important in that they give voice to a segment of the church from which little was heard during this period of time. It is for this reason that in this book, his words will be pushed to the fore. If we care to give him an ear we may yet hear him speak across the generations to our time, calling God's faithful to take up the cause of justice.

CHAPTER ONE

Enslaved in Catholic Kentucky

Daniel Rudd was born in Bardstown, Kentucky, some forty miles southeast of Louisville. Catholics settled this portion of the Bluegrass State making the difficult journey from Maryland in the last decades of the eighteenth century. Church leaders believed this portion of the country would become a leading population center and established the first inland diocese to serve those adventurous pioneers settling the vast territory between the Appalachian Mountains and the Mississippi River. As the community was being established, the inspiring steeple atop the Basilica of St. Joseph Proto-Cathedral was raised; the structure's white columns made up the portico facing the road that ran through the community. Upon the basilica's completion, one observer described the church as the "most stately and capricious house of worship in the state."[1] In the shadow of St. Joseph's steeple a few hundred yards to the southeast, was "Anatok," the estate of Charles and Matilda Haydon. Tax records indicate it was on this farm that young Daniel served as a slave. In 1858 the future editor of the *American Catholic Tribune* was four years old; at the time he was valued at $250.[2]

The Commonwealth of Kentucky permitted its citizens to own slaves. Statistics show many Catholics did traffic in human beings. In 1810, of those living in the state's most populated Catholic region, the Cartwright Creek area, 70 percent would own slaves at some point during their lives.[3] Though some Catholics opposed the so-called "peculiar institution," many saw no conflict of conscience between meeting religious obligations on the one hand and owning slaves on the other. Catholic teaching merely prescribed that slaves be treated humanely. Their religious needs were to be attended to; slaves were to be fed and clothed; and slave owners were not permitted to cruelly beat their charges. There is little evidence, however, to suggest Catholics treated their slaves any more humanely than did the region's non-Catholic population.

Richard Rudd, the slaveholder who owned Daniel's father, Robert Rudd, died in 1833. At the time of Richard's death, his earthly possessions were divided to the satisfaction of the surviving heirs. Included among Richard's earthly possessions was his livestock—33 oxen, 12 horses, 110 hogs, and 89 sheep. Also numbered among the holdings was a group of slaves including Daniel's father, Robert. The entire slave lot was valued at $3,055.[4]

Upon the death of the slaveholder, the fate of Robert and the eleven other slaves was in the hands of the heirs. How much thought went into the well-being of these unfortunate souls at this critical juncture is a matter of conjecture. When the maintenance of the peace among squabbling members of a slaveholding family hung in the balance, oftentimes the familial attachments among slaves were deemed less important. In the case of Daniel's father, it was decided the slaves on Richard's plantation would be divided into four "equal lots" each valuing $763.75. In the final reckoning no special provision was made to keep families together, but in one of the lots it appears that a young mother and her seven-month-old child were indeed portioned off together. In two other lots, however, children under age ten were bequeathed with no adult woman in the group.[5]

Daniel's parents, Robert and Eliza, appear to have been respected in Bardstown's Catholic community. Records indicate Robert likely served as a sponsor to three African Americans baptized into the faith community.[6] Born in 1807, Elizabeth (Eliza) Francis Smith Rudd, Daniel's mother, was known to have been a pious woman.[7] Following Eliza's death, Fr. C. J. O'Connell delayed the funeral service because he wanted to be the one who conducted it. In the memorial service the church leader explained how Elizabeth had received the love and respect of the blacks and whites who knew her. He further declared, "If the colored people followed her saintly example there would be no race problem to vex and fret them."[8]

Despite the respect earned by Robert and Eliza, the institution of slavery placed individuals in bonds in danger of exploitation of the worst kind. Census records indicate both Eliza and her son Daniel were *mulatto*. This term designates one who is of biracial ancestry. Was Eliza the offspring of a biracial relationship? Could Daniel's birth have also been the result of such a union? The consummation of such a relationship was often not mutual. The mulatto designation leaves open the possibility that the Rudd family was forced to live with the ugly scars of sexual exploitation.

Daniel A. Rudd was born into slavery on August 7, 1854. As a result his future was not his own. Rudd's God-given gifts—his dreams and ambitions—would all be subjected to the narrow economic interests of his master. Though he later reflected on his warm experiences in the Catholic Church of his youth, nowhere in the *American Catholic Tribune* during the time he served as its proprietor did Rudd mention the Haydons. And in the 285 extant issues of his newspaper he did not write about his status as a slave. Perhaps the institution was in Rudd's mind so degrading as to discourage any discussion of it. Or it is possible that drawing attention to the fact Rudd's owners were Catholic may have worked against Rudd's editorial agenda. Clues to Rudd's feeling regarding owning slaves can nonetheless be found in select editorials published in the *ACT*.

Rudd advocated for the cause of slave reparations in his newspaper. In an editorial published November 18, 1887, he proposed a reparation plan to direct any surplus funds in the US treasury to former slaves as compensation for their unpaid toil. It would be "a step in the right direction" and would demonstrate the fact that the American people had indeed "repented for the crime of slavery . . . and the countless wrongs done the American Negro," he explained. Rudd concluded that if the money could not be given directly to the survivors, it should be available to educate children in states in which emancipation had left segments of the population in an "abased state."[9]

Despite the inhumanity of such an economic arrangement, it appears the young Rudd was not impeded in his freedom to worship. Rudd's parents and two of his brothers worked as sextons at the Proto-Cathedral in Bardstown. Rudd would later recall that at least one of them was engaged in maintenance duties continuously for sixty-five years. Rudd claimed he had been all over St. Joseph Church from foundation to pinnacle without ever being told to move.[10]

Perhaps Rudd also joined in helping his parents maintain the house of worship. It appears clear that his love of the church was forged in these early years. He would subsequently write of his baptism: "The editor was baptized in

August 1854 at the same font where all the rest, white and black were baptized without discrimination except as who got there first." Rudd expressed the same type of nostalgic sentiment when he spoke of his first communion: "The editor of the Tribune made his first communion there after the long course of study and instruction one must go through with prior to that event and during the time he and all the other Colored and white children sat together and when the late venerable Archbishop Spaulding, then bishop of Louisville . . . administered the sacrament of confirmation, The Tribune man knelt beside as fair a damsel as ever bowed before that rail and thought nothing of it." [11]

Daniel's birth in 1854 coincided with a period of intense polarization in the United States. In this year, the Kansas-Nebraska Act was passed. The legislation essentially dismantled the Missouri Compromise by allowing each future state to vote on whether to enter the Union as a slave or free state. Many northerners were incensed. As slaveholders and opponents of the institution each sought to influence public opinion, clashes became violent. Passions were further enflamed in 1857 when the Dred Scott decision was handed down denying black residents the rights and protections extended to other citizens of the United States.

By Rudd's seventh year the drumbeats of war had reached the peaceful town of Bardstown. In an effort to protect the important, inland port town of Louisville, the Tenth Indiana Infantry Regiment under the command of General Carlos Buell encamped near Rudd's home. The Catholic community was called on to bake bread for the encamped soldiers. By the next spring the college students at St. Joseph College, many of whom held southern sympathies, had fled the campus thus freeing up the remaining Jesuits to work in other areas of ministry. [12]

Closing the doors of the school, Fr. John S. Verdin, SJ, settled on two foci of ministry in need of immediate attention. First, convalescing soldiers from both armies needed medical care. Second, Verdin determined to address the lack of African American involvement in catechetical classes. Prior to this shift in focus, the leader of the Jesuit community had complained "catechetical instruction unsupported by other appeal, made but a feeble impression on the Negro mind." But with the introduction of singing into the programming, which was added in June 1863, attendance increased dramatically.[13] Daniel Rudd received his first communion that month.

Though Rudd did not in any detail reveal his early life in Bardstown, his warm remembrance of Fr. Verdin is telling. After running into him at a gathering in Saint Louis, Rudd wrote, "We had the great pleasure to meet our old instructor. . . . How well did we remember the musical sound of his kind voice. It seemed like childhood days again, when in Bardstown at Old St. Josephs we received words of counsel and listened to his matchless oratory."[14] Whether Verdin was simply Rudd's spiritual instructor or served to teach the young Rudd a more comprehensive course of study is uncertain. In either case, in this caring relationship Rudd appears to have witnessed the best of the Catholic tradition. The editor's early experiences in Bardstown forged within him a positive view of Catholicism. On the other hand, Rudd's nostalgic memories of his days in the church of his youth were, on at least one occasion, called into question by an enquiring Catholic, a Canadian whose name was John L. Smith.[15] In a letter to the editor subsequently published by Rudd, Smith reported he had heard the parish forced black members to sit in segregated seating. Rudd's defense of the church of his youth though vigorous stopped short of denying Smith's claim.[16] Throughout his tenure as the editor of the *American Catholic Tribune* Rudd would work to promote the Catholic Church among African Americans even as he goaded that same church to be more welcoming to members of the black community.

CHAPTER TWO

A Prophetic Voice in a Hope-Filled Season

The Thirteenth Amendment to the United States Constitution brought freedom and hope to those enslaved in the American South. As members of Rudd's family began contemplating a future beyond the bonds of servitude, tragedy visited the home. The Civil War had been over only a few months when Robert, Daniel's father, died. Young Daniel was an impressionable ten years old at the time of his passing. This tragic event may have factored into the family's decision to send Daniel to live with his brother in Springfield, Ohio.

While living with his older brother, Charles Henry, Rudd was afforded the opportunity to complete his schooling in Springfield. Rudd finished his education at the city's old North High School. He also worked at a number of occupations in order to make ends meet. Hoping to better his condition, Rudd moved to Columbus, Ohio, where he lived for a short period. He was likely there from 1879 through 1880, since his name does not appear in the city directory of

Springfield during this period. He had returned to Springfield by 1883.

When Rudd left Bardstown, Kentucky, following the Civil War, he left his mother and several siblings behind; he also left the legacy of slavery in his wake. What he chose to carry with him into his new life was his Catholic faith. While living in Springfield, Rudd found a parish home at St. Raphael Church. This predominantly German church had been founded in 1849 and was the first Catholic Church formed in Greene County, Ohio. Daniel Rudd and his pastor, Fr. William H. Sidley, enjoyed an amiable relationship. Later as publisher of the *American Catholic Tribune*, Rudd was even invited by Sidley to return to the city in order to give a lecture to an integrated gathering of several leading members of the community. This lecture on the history of the church and "her fairness to all mankind" was listened to with "rapt attention." Following the talk, Rudd was happy to report that many in the black community had come to view the church in a new light.[1]

While living in Springfield, Rudd began to agitate on issues related to racial justice. Searching out like-minded individuals Rudd made his influence felt in political circles as he promoted candidates friendly to the aspirations of African Americans. The overwhelming number of black citizens engaged in politics at the time voted Republican, the political party of President Abraham Lincoln who had issued the Emancipation Proclamation. Throughout his career as a journalist, Rudd too showed interest in Republican politics. In this respect he differentiated himself from most of his white coreligionists who were loyal to the Democratic Party. Upon his move to Cincinnati in the summer of 1886, Rudd became an integral member of the Ruffin Club, a Cincinnati-based, black Republican organization. On occasion the group met at the offices of the *ACT*.

A matter constantly confronting people of color was the systemic racial discrimination infecting the state's schools. Though Ohio had remained loyal to the Union during the Civil War, many individuals strongly opposed close racial interaction. African Americans were often forced to attend racially segregated schools. These institutions often lacked the resources available to students attending predominantly white schools. Given this inequity some in the black community sought simply to improve black schools. They did not work for integration because they did not believe school administrators would hire black teachers to teach white children. Rudd, on the other hand, pushed for integration, confident the creation of integrated schools was the best way to achieve racial equality.

In September of 1881, Rudd was propelled to the front line of the struggle for school integration after the children of two of Springfield's black residents were denied entrance into a neighborhood primary school. After African American city leaders decided to challenge the matter in federal court, Rudd was called on to present their cause to Clifton Nichols, a potential financial donor to the initiative. The *Springfield Republic* reported the text of Rudd's speech that apparently swayed Nichols to support the suit. Rudd declared:

> It is pleasant and profitable for us to be here as we are to-night to take steps right and proper for our advancement. Last fall, at the opening of the schools, quite a commotion was created in our midst by a little lady, Miss Eva Gazaway (who I have the pleasure of presenting you), going to the public school in her district and being refused. Her father, doing as none of our citizens have done heretofore, demanded to know why she might not be admitted as well as her next door neighbor, and he was informed that she was black. Hence the reason for the suit and of

our presence here to-night. The citizens met and appointed a committee to carry the case, if necessary, even to the Supreme Court of the United States.

Of individuals, families, and communities our Nation is composed; when all work in harmony and good feeling the general good of the Nation will be secured. This suit is not for Miss Gazaway alone nor for the rights of the children of this community or State, but for all the children.[2]

Though Rudd appears to have been successful in raising the funds necessary to pursue this legal action, the federal court ruled against the petition. The *ACT*'s editor remained undeterred, however. Throughout his publishing career he continued to fight racial segregation in schools, hospitals, and in other public accommodations.

While living in Springfield, Rudd worked with the *Sunday News* and then with the *Review*. He later established the *Ohio State Tribune,* the forerunner to the *ACT*. The visionary editor was a believer in the power of the press. Early in his publishing career he opined, "Editors shape the very destinies of nations."[3] On another occasion Rudd voiced his views on the critical role he believed the press might play in society. He wrote, "If the press would unite in teaching man his moral duty, how much less trouble there would be in the affairs of life."[4]

In the quest for equality and racial justice, newspapers published by African Americans have played a critical role. The first black newspaper printed in the United States was *Freedom's Journal* published from New York. It was founded in 1827 by Samuel Eli Cornish and John Brown Russwurm. Its establishment provided a view of the world from the perspective of a people often disadvantaged by racial prejudice and discrimination. In Rudd's own work one can identify a number of editorial goals similar to those pursued by the publishers of the nation's first black newspaper—to offset misrepresentations of African Americans in the white press; to aid the race in becoming more productive members of society; to promote character development among blacks; and to urge members of the race to fight for their rights, including the right to vote.[5]

Rudd was an enthusiastic member of the Afro-American Press Association. His excitement over the work of the black press is not lost on the reader of his editorials. After the meeting of the press organization in Louisville in 1887, Rudd claimed the group's "harmonious and active work, achieved more good for the race than any convention ever before held by Colored people." He predicted its influence in the future would be strongly felt.[6] Rudd's abilities as the proprietor of the *ACT* did not go unnoticed by his peers in the press. In 1893 he was called on to serve as the chairperson of the Afro-American Press Association. This may have been partly due to his platform for the improvement of this organization. Rudd believed the member newspapers needed to work more closely together to improve quality and save cost. When the Afro-American Press Association was hosted in Cincinnati, the editor proposed the formation of a syndicate to be operated collectively by black newspapers. Rudd again urged this course of action in November of 1891.[7]

Not only was Rudd active in the Afro-American Press Association, but he was also a member of the Catholic Press Association. The editors and proprietors affiliated with this organization held a worldview different from many Protestants working in the mainstream media in the United States. As might be expected, in the *ACT* Rudd was an apologist for the Catholic Church. He believed the church had been ordained by God to promote a justice agenda, one that included the eradication of racial prejudice and discrimination.

But when Catholic leaders failed to live up to the egalitarian teachings of the church, Rudd called on them to live into what he believed to be the cardinal doctrine of the faith, the "Fatherhood of God and Brotherhood of Man." Over time the editor began voicing his view regarding the centrality of the Catholic Church's role in the establishment of justice on behalf of black Americans. The founding of the *American Catholic Tribune* was a platform through which Rudd hoped to influence the public discourse in pursuit of his understanding of justice.

Sometime prior to January 1885, the *Ohio State Tribune*, the forerunner of the *ACT*, was established by Rudd. But the weekly publication did not do well. After recognizing the futility of trying to keep the newspaper going, Rudd decided to reinvent it. Securing a partner in James T. Whitson, a medical doctor who had also served as a principal for a school in Ripley, Ohio, Rudd worked to build a new publication with a modified editorial thrust. But Whitson and Rudd did not work well together, and soon after the partnership ended in acrimony. What the nature of their disagreement was is unclear. Rudd subsequently bought Whitson's share of the publication.[8]

Now alone, Rudd pressed ahead with his vision for the new publication. He continued a number of editorial objectives he had promoted in his former newspaper. Indeed Rudd did report on the important news of the day. At times he also editorialized on significant matters being discussed around the country. One such editorial was occasioned by the tragic Johnstown Flood, which took the lives of more than two thousand people. Movingly he wrote,

> Never before in the history of our country, has such calamity befall[en] . . . its people, as the recent horror of Johnstown. No pen or camera can portray the awful catastrophe

The real number of human lives that were swallowed up in surging floods or burned out in the pyre at the bridge will not be known until that fearful day when all the sons of Adam stand before God's judgment. Yet the groans and shrieks of the dying, the lamentations of the rescued and the silent appeal of the dead, have opened the well-springs of Christian charity and sympathy.[9]

A second objective carried over from the *Ohio State Tribune* was related to the editor's desire to "fight for the eternal principles of liberty, justice, and equality before the law." How this goal was to be attained shifted, however. Beginning with the establishment of the *ACT*, Rudd promoted the church as central to the work of justice in the United States. He sought to "give the great Catholic Church a hearing and show" that it was "worthy of at least a fair consideration at the hands of [the] race." Rudd further claimed the Catholic Church was "the only place on the Continent, where rich and poor, white and black, must drop prejudice at the threshold and go hand in hand to the altar." Reflecting on his decision to create the *ACT*, Rudd on another occasion said, "I have always been a Catholic and, feeling that I knew the teachings of the Catholic church [sic], I thought there could be no greater factor in solving the race problem than that matchless institution whose history for 1900 years is but a continual triumph over all assailants." Rudd's conviction about the role the Catholic Church might play in the uplift of the race was certainly part of the reason he established the *ACT*. Rudd also was a savvy businessman. It is likely the advantages of establishing a newspaper with an unserved niche market did not escape his notice.[10]

The reasoning behind Rudd's choice to move the *ACT* to Cincinnati is something of a mystery. The city was populated with many individuals with less than progressive views on the plight of the nation's former bondsmen. But Cincinnati had played home to black newspapers before Rudd's arrival in 1886. *The Colored Citizen* of Cincinnati was one of the nation's few black newspapers published during the Civil War era. The *Declaration*, Charles W. Bell's newspaper, was sold in Cincinnati through the 1870s. The *Colored Patriot*, a Republican newspaper, followed Bell's publication. Since the city had hosted a number of race papers prior to his coming, perhaps Rudd believed he would find enough local supporters to help launch a national newspaper with readers from all across the country. It is likely the editor's decision to move was also strongly influenced by the support he received from William H. Elder, archbishop of Cincinnati. Rudd routinely printed the following endorsement given by this church leader: "I am very much pleased with the great labor you are applying to make The American Catholic Tribune a useful and interesting factor in advancing the best interests not only of your own immediate people, but of the whole country. And I am glad to see your very satisfactory success, and to learn of your steady progress. You are obtaining for yourselves both the esteem of your readers, and the blessing of God. I give you my blessing."[11]

In an editorial Rudd trumpeted the growing reach of his newspaper:

> In New York and New England our business manager has been received in a manner worthy of the cause. In Maryland, Virginia, New Jersey, the District of Columbia, West Virginia, Kentucky and Ohio, our representatives report the most hearty receptions. From Indiana, Michigan, Illinois and Missouri come the same glad tiding. The far West and South send us good news. In the Carolinas, Tennessee, Georgia Alabama, Florida, Mississippi and Louisiana receive the American Catholic Tribune as the advocate of right and

justice. We promised the race a National journal and our
Catholic friends especially with all the other friends of the
race in general are helping to do so.[12]

In terms of structure the setup of Rudd's newspaper was
not much different than other newspapers of the day. The
ACT was four pages in length and offered six or seven
columns of print per page. In this respect the newspaper
resembled other important race papers including *The Washington Bee* and the *Cleveland Gazette*.[13] What distinguished
Rudd's weekly from other newspapers of the era was its
staunchly pro-Catholic editorial perspective.

The primary target audience for Rudd's newspaper was
the African American reading public. Yet it is likely the read-
ership of the *ACT* included as many whites as it did African
Americans. As Joseph Lackner has pointed out, the types of
products regularly advertised in black newspapers were
largely absent from the advertisement columns printed in
the *ACT*. Still, Rudd asked Caucasians who came to his
public lectures to contribute to his newspaper so that copies
of the publication could be shared with black readers.[14]

Early in the life of the *ACT* Rudd sometimes ran short of
the funds needed to keep his publishing operation solvent.
In one edition he complained that one of the hardest aspects
of the job of a proprietor of an African American newspaper
was spending time trying to secure the funds to keep the
publication in the black. To this end Rudd worked diligently.
Over time the editor's hard work paid off.[15]

A source of revenue beyond the money raised in subscrip-
tion sales came from Catholic church members who strongly
believed both in Rudd and his missionary efforts on behalf
of African Americans. The church stood to reap a huge
harvest of souls should it open its arms to the nation's re-

cently emancipated and much abused population, Rudd contended. "The American Catholic Tribune is a perpetual mission, and every dollar given or extended for it is a help in the mission," Rudd wrote.[16] His efforts at collecting funds from well-to-do Catholics did not always prove successful, yet many of his coreligionists supported his evangelistic passion. One such supporter of the newspaper was Msgr. John E. Burke who at one time served as the pastor of St. Benedict the Moor Church in New York City. After a presentation by Rudd at this church, Burke offered the following endorsement, "I will act as an agent for the American Catholic Tribune and propose to help him otherwise. I will not ask you to give me a collection for him, but I do want to take his paper and pay him for it. I have been taking it for two years and gladly recommend it. I now give Mr. Rudd as a donation to the cause fifty dollars. I do not give it for him, but for his paper. It is no charity for him, but it is an aid to his noble efforts."[17]

Upon his arrival in Cincinnati in 1886, Rudd and partner James T. Whitson set up a printing business at 233 West Fourth Street, near the city's business district. The company printed, among other requested items, custom cards, letterheads, envelopes, billheads, statements, pamphlets, books, and briefs. The revenue from this business aided Rudd in the publication of the *ACT*. Over time the enterprise expanded and the business relocated to a more suitable location.

Throughout its eleven-year run, the *ACT* was primarily marketed to a domestic audience. Nevertheless it caught the attention of Catholics living beyond the borders of the United States. For example, Bishop Pedro Schumacher, C. M., of Portoviejo in Ecuador, endorsed Rudd's paper. This church leader thought the *ACT* might enjoy even more success in the church if it were translated into Spanish. In

August of 1887, the newspaper embarked on a second year
of publication. At this juncture Rudd claimed the *ACT* was
being read every week in Europe.[18]

After settling in Cincinnati, Rudd attempted to establish
a printing school at the *ACT* plant. The editor intended to
apprentice both young women and young men. Though it
is unlikely that much revenue was generated from the initiative, Rudd was a big believer in vocational training. Because
of the paper's modest start, the editor could not take on as
many students as he had hoped. In August of 1888, however,
he again voiced his intention of bringing on more understud-
ies. In pursuit of this goal, Rudd urged his readers to sub-
scribe to the *ACT*. The increased revenue would make it
possible for him to establish the school. At the time Rudd
was willing to take on individuals who could do composi-
tion, presswork, and every other position in the field, from
reporting to telegraphy. His effort at establishing a strong
vocational school increased dramatically in 1892, just prior
to the paper's move to Detroit.

By early 1891 the ambitious Rudd had made the decision
to publish the *ACT* from both Chicago and Cincinnati. He
no doubt believed such a move would open a new market
for the newspaper. Lincoln Valle, Rudd's longtime associate,
served as the city editor. News from the Windy City was
conspicuously reported in issues of the *ACT* published at
this time. While Rudd was attempting to make a home for
the *ACT* in Chicago, he and his staff developed a closer
partnership with the nation's first priest open about his African American heritage, Fr. Augustus Tolton. At the time
Tolton was working earnestly to raise funds in order to build
a new parish in Chicago. Rudd supported the effort and
donated to the cause. Tolton reciprocated. He told Rudd he
planned to make the *ACT* the official newspaper of the new

parish, expressing a genuine affection for both Valle and Rudd.

Rudd and Tolton shared a common goal. Both leaders sought to minister to African Americans, many of whom had been forced to the margins of American society because of the country's structural inequities. Even the church had been complicit. Both of these gifted leaders held out hope the institution would rediscover its missional responsibility to its African American members. For as Rudd confidently declared, only the Catholic Church can "solve the Negro Problem on right lines." He believed this could be done only by making the black race the "absolute social and political equal of every other race."[19]

CHAPTER THREE

Finding Justice in the Catholic Church

Evidence from the *American Catholic Tribune* shows Rudd was active politically. Revealing a pragmatic streak, he believed the rights of African Americans and Catholics needed to be protected by politicians. While residing in Cincinnati, Rudd was an involved member of the Ruffin Club, a black Republican organization. Sometimes he energetically campaigned either for or against candidates seeking political office. For example on one occasion, Rudd used the *ACT* to discredit an Ohio district representative who was in league with the American Protective Association (APA), an anti-Catholic organization. Rudd accused this candidate of fighting against three more deserving competitors. He further noted that individuals seeking to "bring about Religious strife" between citizens were "unworthy of respectful consideration."[1]

After Rudd began publishing the *ACT*, his political activism remained, though it was eclipsed by his promotion of the Catholic Church. In the late winter of 1888, he expressed the reason for this new, modified, church-centered activism: "Political parties have all failed to do the Negro anything like justice. The Republican Party with all the prestige of victory to back them were in power for twenty years after that victory and did much talking and promising but in the end, when a rotten public opinion held up its hand in wholly [sic] horror at the appearance of equal citizenship, it dropped behind that cowardly subterfuge the tariff, and an outraged and disgusted people hurried that party from power and placed the reins of government in the hands of the Democracy."[2]

Rudd began to promote the Catholic Church as the divine agent predestined to play a central role in fighting the injustice of racism in Jim Crow America. In the editor's view, the church was a universal organization and one unpolluted by America's misguided obsession with skin color. As Rudd travelled the country, he championed the merits of the Catholic Church urging black Americans to enter its fold. This divine institution, he argued, had from its beginning been engaged in the promotion of equality. As he looked back over history, he recognized the church as the primary agent of positive change with a legacy of lifting the oppressed in every age. This work of elevation had in Rudd's own generation again borne fruit, the emancipation of the nation's enslaved population.

It is possible to discern in Rudd's writing a Catholic hermeneutic for reading history and one common among apologists of Rudd's era—the romantic apologetic for Catholicism. In short, individuals who viewed history through this lens claimed that the Catholic Church had been the principle agent for the growth and development of Western Civilization. The preservation of texts, advancements in the arts, the improved treatment of women, and the abolishment of serfdom in Europe were all positive developments resulting from the witness and ministry of the church over

many centuries. On the other hand, Protestants often promoted a very different reading of history. They believed the
Catholic Church had more often than not opposed forces
of liberty and progress. In the minds of many Protestant
thinkers, it was the overthrow of Catholic hegemony in the
sixteenth century that allowed the rich fruit of present civilization to ripen.

Holding to a Catholic view of reading the past, Rudd on
one occasion wrote, "Anyone who has read history and
given ear to the inevitable conclusions that grow out of its
teachings, can see at a glance that in the Catholic Church
alone is the only permanent advancement to be made. She
alone advances steadily, and in her upward flight, carries
with her all the races of mankind on an equal footing."[3]

Employing an example of this spirit of progress, Rudd
highlighted the interracial fellowship occurring at St. Ann's
Parish, his home church. He wrote, "There, too, may be seen
people of every complexion from white to black, of every
tongue spoken in this great cosmopolitan town, of every
shade of wealth, all kneeling side by side or approaching
the communion table side by side."[4]

Early in the life of the *American Catholic Tribune*, the
masthead of the newspaper boasted an engraving of the
pope surrounded by a diverse group of faithful church members representing various ethnicities and nationalities. What
is clearly being communicated in the masthead is the universal and diverse character of the church's membership.
This aspect of the church's essential constitution was one
Rudd systematically attempted to highlight. For the editor,
the Catholic Church had a unique and essential role to play
in society. In his mind this divine institution was the only
organization that knew "no east, no west, no north, no
south, no race, no color."[5] Rudd's ecclesiology communi-

cated an equality and sense of unity he believed would offer an alternative to the bigotry and division so prevalent in American society.

Rudd sometimes brought to the attention of his readers integrated churches where equality among members was a distinguishing feature. The existence of these egalitarian fellowships offered proof of the church's authenticity. For example on a trip to Mobile, Alabama, Rudd was encouraged to find black and white Catholics worshiping together. His experience led him to label the fellowship the "one Apostolic church." In this same parish, Rudd noted that "the color of a man's skin does not bar him from mingling with the whites at the communion railing, nor does it bar him from any seat in that church."[6]

Rudd believed the Catholic Church provided a welcome sanctuary for the often-mistreated members of the race. Within her gates black members would be received as equals—brothers and sisters in the Lord. Trumpeting his vision of an egalitarian and integrated faith community, Rudd traveled the country emphasizing his conviction that the Catholic Church was indeed the best hope for African Americans. In a speech delivered by Rudd in Celtic Hall in Pawtucket, Rhode Island, the editor spoke of the condition of the race in the South. He drew attention to the "industry and economy" of the African American population, and to the advancement of the race since emancipation. On the other hand, Rudd did not attempt to hide what he said was the "deplorable condition" of his people in the South. Roughly nine million individuals who had formerly lived in forced servitude, he explained, were suffering under a "withering blight of ignorance and superstition." For Rudd the solution was relatively simple—the education of the hand and heart. In his estimation only the Catholic Church could apply this same remedy.[7]

Rudd did not believe Protestants would receive African Americans into their denominational fellowships as equals. In the Catholic Church, he contended, little racial prejudice could be found. On the other hand, in Protestant churches, he claimed black members were routinely being forced to sit in segregated seating. Highlighting the ill treatment members of the race were receiving in Protestant churches, Rudd wrote, "It would be amusing if it were not so serious, to watch our people catching at the various versions of Protestant belief, when at every turn they are met with a cold shoulder and told in the most insulting terms that 'no nigger need apply.' "[8]

Rudd recognized that other Christian groups were preaching the brotherhood of humanity under God. But he didn't see this same egalitarian rhetoric being lived out in these various communities of faith. On occasion Rudd singled out denominational groups for treating black churchgoers unjustly. In 1889 he took members of an Episcopal convention to task after a motion to receive black churchgoers on terms of equality was ruled out of order. Rudd also criticized Presbyterians for not having the right sort of Christianity. Rudd could count only two Presbyterians of color in Cincinnati. Rudd also criticized the treatment black members were receiving in Methodist churches. On at least one occasion, Rudd's paper took aim at a champion of evangelical Christianity, famed revivalist Dwight L. Moody. This article, copied from another newspaper, took to task the dynamic leader for not addressing the sin of racism during a meeting he had recently held in Louisville. In summation, Rudd was certainly correct in his criticism of the racial discrimination prevalent in Protestant churches. Rudd's polemics against denominational churches, however, minimized incidents of discrimination toward African Americans within his own, beloved Catholic community of faith.

Rudd's praise of the Catholic Church's treatment of African Americans appears a bit too generous at times. Obviously he encountered racial prejudice within the Catholic fold. Some examples of discrimination strike the reader of the *ACT* as blatantly obvious. On occasion even the idealistic editor was forced to acknowledge the presence of bigoted individuals among the Catholic faithful. But when encountering prejudiced Catholics, Rudd was quick to distinguish their bad, individual behavior from the official teachings of the church. Racist Catholics had not learned prejudice from the doctors of the church; they were simply bad Catholics, Rudd argued. On one rare occasion Rudd took aim at those within the church harboring racist ideas. He warned that churchgoers guilty of mistreating people on the basis of race were less than Catholics. Moreover, they could expect someday to give an account for their behavior. He wrote, "There is no race problem in this country except as it exists in the pampered prejudices of either narrow minded, ignorant or uncharitable people. . . . There is no room in heaven for prejudice, and people had better come to that conclusion here than to suffer hereafter."[9]

In the pages of the *ACT,* Rudd encouraged his Catholic readers (many of whom were white) to create faith communities more welcoming to African Americans. He urged Catholics to model kind treatment, to drop racial prejudice at the door of the church, and to be intentional about leading persons from the black community into the Catholic family of faith. In the *ACT,* Rudd explained how he had many times been questioned as to how to bring African Americans into the Catholic Church. Catholic institutions founded for black constituents should be promoted, he explained. He also expressed the need to support the work of the Oblate Sisters of Providence at Baltimore, Saint Louis, and Leavenworth, as well as that of the Sisters of the Holy Family at New Orleans, whose covent had been previously damaged in a fire. Where there were black schools hiring secular teachers, Rudd explained these hires needed to be members of the race. Not surprisingly, Rudd urged his coreligionists to support the black Catholic press. He also instructed his readers to encourage members of the African American community to be independent and to do for themselves.

Rudd at times found himself having to answer correspondence from individuals challenging his more generous appraisal of the church's treatment of African Americans. For example, the editor of the *Sentinel*, a Pennsylvania newspaper, questioned Rudd as to why so few black priests were serving the church in the United States. Rudd responded to this challenge by arguing the Catholic Church spent more than any other denomination educating African Americans. He also drew attention to the work of St. Peter Claver, a seventeenth-century, Spanish, Jesuit who worked among enslaved persons in Columbia and who some mistakenly believed to be of African origin. In this same defense Rudd drew attention to the ministry of Augustus Tolton, who was ordained the same year the editor founded the *ACT*. Finally, he highlighted the work of Archbishop Francis Janssens, who previously advocated for the training of black priests and teachers.

On another occasion the *People's Advocate* of Washington, DC, questioned Rudd's portrayal of the church's egalitarian relationship to its African American membership. The creation of St. Joseph Seminary in Baltimore, a separate institution with a mandate to train black clergy, gave the appearance the aspirants were being racially segregated. Rudd was called on to explain this apparent contradiction. To the editor's credit, he did not shy away from questions of this type. He explained that different religious societies have each their own rules of discipline and purpose. St. Joseph Seminary existed to train black clergy. Thus it was not created to segregate black aspirants.

Rudd's advocacy for Catholicism was in part fueled by his conviction that society over the generations would be made more just through the teaching ministry of the Catholic Church. This leavening, the fruits of which were apparent in Rudd's era, was a continuation of a divinely sanctioned mission being carried forward by the church from its inception nineteen thousand years earlier. Rudd counted on the church to teach society a respect for God and love for neighbor. Further he claimed the "Fatherhood of God and Brotherhood of Man" was central to the message of the gospel. This foundational Christian truth had been communicated in the biblical record beginning with the creation account in Genesis. The creation narrative offered a theological underpinning for Rudd's convictions regarding the equality and essential worth of all people. Perhaps the editor's strong stand against the teaching of biological evolution reveals a belief that this same scientific theory threatened to undermine an essential theological foundation for his egalitarian convictions.

Rudd's defense of the Catholic Church's relationship to the African American community may have been at times polemical in character. Still Rudd and others found evidence of the church's good will toward African Americans. During the years he published the *ACT*, he continued to view the Catholic Church as a sincere partner in society's quest for equality and justice.

CHAPTER FOUR

Partners in Pursuit of Equality

In the last decades of the nineteenth century, the editor of the *American Catholic Tribune* found reason to believe the Catholic Church could be counted on as an ally in the cause of justice. This confidence was fueled in part by the broad range of ministry efforts initiated on behalf of the African American community. Rudd's confidence in the church's goodwill had taken root during his early years in Bardstown. But the editor's positive encounters with church leaders did not end when he left the town of his birth. As an adult when he took up the task of creating the *American Catholic Tribune,* he found much needed support among Catholic clergymen. His efforts to launch the Colored Catholic Congress movement likewise received the approbation of ranking church leaders including bishops. Rudd also was called on to aid in the planning of the first Congress of Lay Catholics in 1889.

As mentioned previously, Cardinal James Gibbons supported Rudd's evangelistic efforts among black women and men. The head of the American Catholic Church even made room in his schedule to address the first Colored Catholic Congress gathering held in Washington, DC, in 1889. Other ranking church officials joined Rudd's effort offering financial help and endorsements.

Efforts to recruit, train, and ordain black clergy provided Rudd with further proof of the church's commitment to African Americans, even though at times these same American church leaders seemed to drag their feet in the face of Rome's advocacy for black vocations. During Rudd's era, John R. Slattery and the American Josephites deserve much of the credit for the work of training black clergymen. Even so the road to the priesthood for black aspirants was a tough one. Efforts to place them in parishes, particularly in the South, were met by reluctant clergy as well as members of the laity. Sadly only a handful of black priests were ordained during Rudd's lifetime. This fact did not keep him from celebrating the ministry of those African Americans who were ordained by the church including Augustus Tolton. Rudd featured an oversized engraving of the priest in one of the issues of the *ACT*. In another he advertised the sale of photos of this churchman.

For the editor the very existence of a black Catholic priest proved the sincerity of the church's commitment to equality. Tolton's ordination also challenged racist ideology with regard to the inferiority of African Americans, a prejudicial feeling prevalent in American society in Rudd's era. Moreover the elevation of Tolton directly countered those in the community who believed black men to be morally unfit to serve this high office. Rudd communicated his sentiments about Tolton and the church's willingness to ordain persons of color in an editorial penned in 1888: "The Catholic Church takes men from all the walks of life and if they but follow her example and teachings she will not only place them beyond the railings, but she will guarantee them a sure footing and endless happiness in the world beyond the grave."[1]

The benevolence and charitable ministry of St. Katharine Drexel offered further evidence of Catholicism's commitment to the African American community. She and the religious order she founded, the Sisters of the Blessed Sacrament, established schools across the country for the benefit of black youth. Because people of color were being denied entrance into Catholic schools, this educational ministry was particularly important. On occasion Rudd defended the religious order's work. Such a defense was necessary in part because some southern Catholics argued that the promotion of religion among the black population was a waste of money. Critics argued that these benevolent monies should have been spent on members of Drexel's own race.

Several instances are recorded in the *ACT* in which a fraternal spirit existing among Catholics of goodwill seemed to transcend racial differences. For example, Rudd's reception into the Catholic press organization left him with a positive view of his white coreligionists. After attending the second gathering of this assembly in New York in 1891, Rudd wrote, "The events of the past week, have again proven that the Catholic Church ignores the color line. She has none and does not want one. Those who try so persistently to show that she has one, or to make one for her, are shams and failures."[2] The following year Rudd was given the honor of addressing this same assembly.

Another telling encounter that helped to form Rudd's positive view of fellow Catholics occurred after the editor received an invitation to attend the fifth annual gathering of the Catholic Knights of America. The meeting was held in Covington, Kentucky, right across the river from Rudd's Cincinnati-based operation. Representatives from thirty-six branches of the organization gathered from all parts of the Bluegrass State. Several prominent citizens as well as members of the Catholic clergy dignified the meeting. A banquet was scheduled for those attending the gathering. Rudd was asked to be one of the speakers. A man of Jewish heritage, Geza Berger, was also invited. A commotion, however, was raised when Dr. Henry DeGruyter, a representative of one of the city's German newspapers, informed the committee on arrangements that he thought it beneath him to sit at a table with a Jew and a "Negro." DeGruyter's response caught the organizers by surprise. An emergency meeting was called to settle the matter. The next day the committee on arrangements determined Dr. DeGruyter was guilty of gross "impertinence" because he had attempted to dictate whom the Knights could select as guests and associates. It was decided the Knights could not recognize distinction of race or color. It was further determined Dr. DeGruyter's invitation would be rescinded.[3]

At the banquet the previously arranged program was followed, and Rudd was called on to speak. The gentleman who introduced him explained the unfortunate incident. When Rudd's name was subsequently announced to the gathering, a grand ovation erupted all across the hall. "It was an ovation a prince would be proud of," Rudd later wrote. The editor's speech was "scholarly and dignified," the article reported. Rudd's statement detailing the pride he felt in addressing the assembly as "brother Catholics" again brought an eruption of applause. His reception by this group made a marked impression. Rudd would later write, "The Catholic Knight[s] of America are true to Catholic teachings. The Catholics of Covington smashed the color line in a most noble manner. All honor to such a noble minded, big-hearted people, May God bless them."[4]

In 1890 the *ACT* began reporting on the ministry of Archbishop John Ireland of Saint Paul, Minnesota. This charismatic leader was an influential representative of the Catholic Church in the United States. Known for his sometimes controversial positions, the church leader's contentious comments on race relations were beginning to gain the ear of individuals both within the Catholic Church and beyond. As it turned out, Rudd found much he appreciated in Ireland's words. In some ways the prelate gave voice to Rudd's own views on racial equality and justice. The prelate's progressive ideas also found many cheerleaders among black Americans. The fact that Ireland was a ranking official in the Catholic Church made it easier for Rudd to promote the faith among people of color. The church leader's progressive position on equality and the color line, Rudd would subsequently suggest, was in fact the official teaching of the church.

Archbishop Ireland had been a chaplain in the Union Army during the US Civil War. His push for the recognition of the full social equality of African Americans was radical. While some in the church favored equal treatment before the courts (legal equality), or more job opportunities (economic equality), or the removal of the color line in public accommodations (equality in public accommodations), very few called for the recognition of the full social equality of African Americans, a position that essentially eradicated the color line even in the most intimate relations. Ireland's understanding of social equality even tacitly sanctioned interracial marriage. Many viewed these unions as illicit. Predictably Ireland's views scandalized many inside and outside the Catholic Church. But Rudd latched on to Ireland's public statements on matters of race. The archbishop was saying what black listeners wanted to hear. Though many in the black community would have disapproved of interracial marriage, they nonetheless viewed Ireland's position as more dignifying to people of color. Rudd made use of the archbishop's views to show the church's friendliness to the cause of African Americans. Because of the importance of Ireland to black Catholics in the nineteenth century, his words and work merit further study.

Evidence from the *ACT* shows Rudd began following Ireland's statements on race and the color line in the spring of 1890. The editor reported on a series of sermons given by the churchman and two of his associates at an event to help raise funds for the erection of a black parish in Saint Paul. Though Ireland headed up the groundbreaking, two of his like-minded priests joined him in the effort: Fr. John Gmeiner and Fr. John T. Harrison. The words delivered at this festive gathering expressed a more robust and fuller expression of equality—one that appealed to African Americans. Father John Gmeiner played down the differences between whites and blacks. He claimed there were no essential differences between the races. Differences that did exist were merely accidental. Though this progressive priest acknowledged that African Americans had yet to reach the full height of modern civilization, he placed the blame for this fact on the dilatory effect of the institution of slavery. Father Gmeiner drew attention to the marked progress black Americans had made in the decades since emancipation.[5]

Rather than saddling the race with some inadequacy, Archbishop Ireland identified racial prejudice as the root cause of the race problem. This racism was incongruent with either American citizenship or Christianity. The archbishop claimed, "We are not merely all Americans, we are all Christians, and the cardinal principle of religion is one brotherhood for all men." "Christ died for all; we are all laved in the same Baptismal waters, and the hope of heaven is extended to all," Ireland asserted. "How one Christian can repel from his side another simply because he is of a different color, passes my understanding," he said. Ireland argued that slavery had been used as the excuse for not extending equality to individuals who had formerly been enslaved. He believed the culpability of the country for this dehumanizing institution needed to be hurriedly remediated by conveying the full complement of rights on African Americans. Even more remarkably, he urged equality not only in matters civil and legal, but also in social relations. Finally Ireland's suggestion for dealing with the race problem was to "obliterate absolutely all color line." The archbishop encouraged African Americans to take refuge in the Catholic Church. Within her sanctuary, he promised, they would find justice. In an act of boldness before the gathering, he claimed no "negro problem" existed. I "know no color line, I acknowledge none," he asserted.[6]

Ireland recognized his position on race relations would not be well received by certain segments of the population. Yet he believed he was right in taking this principled stand. Though his view on racial equality seemed "untimely to-day," it would nonetheless be "to-morrow timely," he declared. His fault he speculated was that he was simply "ahead of his day." He predicted a time in the future, however, when Americans would wonder why race prejudice ever existed.[7]

The next month the archbishop agreed to deliver a sermon for Fr. Michael J. Walsh, rector of St. Augustine Parish in Washington, DC. Ireland appears to have sought this opportunity because he wanted to help steer the dialogue on race relations in a more progressive direction. He agreed to come to St. Augustine on the condition his sermon would be published in the *Catholic Mirror*. On the Sunday Ireland spoke, the church was filled with parishioners as well as ranking government officials. Ireland took full advantage of the opportunity to disseminate his egalitarian views.

Ireland's controversial message placed those in the audience under obligation to address racial inequality. In the hearing of representatives of the federal government, he urged America to make amends for slavery by recognizing the rights of African Americans. He spoke to his fellow churchmen reminding them the cornerstone of Catholic teaching was the "equality of all men." Ireland called on his hearers to "look one another in the face as members of the same family, children of the same God." "No church is a fit temple of God where a man because his color is excluded or made to occupy a corner," he continued. As for the color line being drawn across society, he said it should be removed directly. The line between individuals should be drawn only on "personal merit."[8]

In his moving sermon Ireland seized the opportunity to address both white and black Catholics. When white Catholics succumbed to race prejudice, he explained, they were contradicting God's teachings as to equality and fraternity. He urged his white coreligionists to "extend the right hand of fellowship to their Colored brethren." Among Catholics "there was not and could not be a color question." Speaking to African Americans in the audience, the prelate urged patience. He encouraged these same hearers to show themselves worthy of the equality due them. Finally he encouraged his black listeners to "judiciously and sternly" "stand for their rights."[9]

Archbishop Ireland's sermon was published in the *Catholic Mirror*. Prefacing the watershed message was the following introduction:

We have long wished for an ending to the discussion of the Negro question, but we cannot reach the end until the matter is settled and settled right. The venerable archbishop

of St. Paul preached a sermon in Washington recently that
has awakened the deepest interest in everything that per-
tains to the conversion of the Negro as well as to show
conclusively that the race prejudice is a crime that we must
as Catholics, lift ourselves above it or go down under Just
retribution.[10]

Rudd was clearly emboldened by Ireland's sermon. He
declared it to be a "magnificent demand for simple justice."[11]
On another occasion he called the address a "masterly plea
for justice."[12] Following the sermon's publication Rudd remarked, "If the Colored Press of the United States means to
be fair to the race and the cause of equality the sermon of
Archbishop Ireland will be reproduced in every Negro paper
in the United States. . . . Justice must and will prevail."[13]

Several papers, Catholic and Protestant alike, responded
to Ireland's comments. The *Catholic Mirror* offered the following: "The equality of all men, in the eyes of the Common
Father of mankind, can not for one moment be questioned
by a follower of Jesus Christ." The Catholic Church does
not draw the color line, *The Catholic Columbian* reported.[14]
Black newspapers responded favorably to the archbishop's
sermon as well. *The Washington Bee* broadcast its conviction that the Catholic Church was the "first to extend the
hand of fellowship and declare in favor of a universal
brotherhood and equality."[15] Thomas Fortune's *New York
Age* commented on the "startling truths" in the church
leader's "remarkable sermon" on "Social Equality." What
was of special note to the columnist was the promise "absolute social and religious" equality would be recognized
within the Catholic Church.[16]

Ireland's sermon gave public voice to Rudd's own desire
to see the absolute removal of the color line being drawn in
America's churches as well as in society. During the years

Rudd published the *ACT*, he seems to have had little patience for members of the race who might have been contented with less. In one instance Rudd quoted an exchange from the *Justice* of Chattanooga in which a southerner, likely an African American contributor, claimed black citizens merely wanted equality before the law. The color line, the writer acknowledged, was simply too indelibly drawn and could be expected to continue to divide the races in church, family, and marriage. Rudd was incensed with this suggestion. He labeled the idea "driveling nonsense." One who would write such material, he continued, ought to rightly hide himself from the public forever.[17]

Support for the recognition of the full equality of African Americans often hinged on whether interracial marriages ought to be permitted. The overwhelming majority of whites inside and outside the church believed the white race to be superior to the "Negro Race." To allow interracial unions was to risk the pollution of the dominant race. Some African Americans also firmly opposed interracial unions, though members of the black community held their own cultural reasons for doing so. The fullest expression of social equality, however, seemed to necessitate the removal of the color line even in the most intimate of social relationships.

Rudd did not take a strong public stand on the right of African Americans and whites to marry. Possible reasons for reticence on Rudd's part are obvious. From the editor's perspective, it may have been the large numbers of people who would have protested a progressive stand on marriage. Some of these opponents held influential positions in the church. Father John M. Mackey (later a monsignor), for example, strongly disdained the practice of what he termed "amalgamation." On the other hand, Rudd drew attention to members of the Catholic clergy including Archbishop

Francis Janssens who condemned legislation barring inter-racial marriage. Rudd also was not shy in his general criticism of newspapers opposed to the practice, including the *Adam* of Memphis.

Opposition to Ireland's call for the immediate recognition of the full social equality of African Americans and the requisite removal of the color line was widely criticized. Even in the northern part of the country, Ireland's position was viewed as radical. Archbishop Patrick John Ryan of Philadelphia, a supporter of Rudd's newspaper, voiced his disapproval of Ireland's stand. In a letter to Archbishop Michael Augustine Corrigan of New York, he wrote, "Archbishop Ireland has created a sensation in Washington and through the country, by declaring that Catholics should admit negroes to social as well as political and religious equality. His enthusiasm sometimes leads him too far, but his purity of intention is unquestionable. Social equality is always the last attained, and only time and merit on the part of the Negroes can affect it."[18]

Even more surprising was Fr. Mackey's opposition to Ireland's stand against the removal of the color line. The pastor's thinly veiled rebuttal of Ireland's sermon was delivered in what appears in hindsight to be an ill-advised setting. Mackey played host to the Colored Catholic Congress in Cincinnati in July 1890, only about two months after the archbishop's sermon was published. Though Ireland's name was never invoked in his opening address, Mackey's meaning would have been clear enough to the delegates in attendance. The church leader declared, "The white race does not desire amalgamation with the Negro race. The individual of either race who disregards this line of demarcation drawn apparently by nature herself, is no credit to either race. The races will go down the stream of time to the end on parallel lines as they have reached us, equal in the Fatherhood of God and Brotherhood of Man."[19]

Interestingly delegates to the congress didn't seem to have taken Mackey's comments sitting down. Before the end of the meeting, their host was put on the defensive. On matters of race he seems to have retreated, declaring that he was "squarely on the same platform with Archbishop Ireland."[20]

The allies within the Catholic Church who supported Rudd encouraged him and likeminded activists to push the cause of justice forward. For Rudd the primary instrument he used in this campaign was his newspaper, the *American Catholic Tribune*. Throughout its life he employed it to defend the dignity and rights of the African American community.

CHAPTER FIVE

A Foundation for Justice

Foundational to Rudd's advocacy for the full equality of African Americans was his campaign to support the dignity of the race. During the years of the *American Catholic Tribune*'s publication, the editor routinely found himself challenging individuals who believed African Americans to be inferior to white Americans—biologically, intellectually, and morally. Even science was sometimes called upon to support this racist ideology. Rudd's task was no doubt a frustrating one. Over time he would discover that even his allies in the campaign for justice needed to be disabused of errant notions about the black community. Rudd's campaign in support of the dignity of members of the African American community did more than challenge racist ideas among whites; it also served to encourage black women and men who were being inundated with a steady diet of negative messages about people of color.

In the same month Rudd founded the *ACT*, the editor spoke out against the discrimination and caste prejudice that he claimed were "ever bobbing up to thwart the American Negro in his manly efforts to make himself an honest and upright citizen." The chief cause of the unjust race relations in the United States, Rudd reasoned, was that "one class" had always been taught that they were better than the other. Moreover he insisted that "people who [know] otherwise had rather submit to the injustice than worry themselves enough to correct the evil." But Rudd wasn't one to sit idly by. He sought to challenge stereotypical views of members of the black community because these same negative beliefs were the rationale behind Jim Crow segregation.[1]

Rudd employed the power of the pen to defend the dignity of African Americans. In 1892 he published a rebuttal to what appears to have been a demeaning portrayal of the race written by Rabbi Edward N. Calisch of Richmond, Virginia. To these criticisms Rudd responded with sarcasm, "The Rabbi's knowledge of the Afro American is about on par with the knowledge of nine-tenths [of] all the other white men who take up their little pens to solve the 'Negro Problem?' He has met some barbers, some Pullman car porters and some hotel waiters. Then he has probably stood outside or perhaps inside of some church where some ignorant Afro American preacher has 'explained the Bible,' the words of which he could neither pronounce or define." If the Rabbi were to visit one of the homes of African Americans in Richmond or any other locality, he would likely form a different opinion, Rudd reasoned.[2]

On another occasion Rudd voiced his displeasure about how some black marchers had been demeaned by the manner in which they participated in a parade celebrating the nation's centennial. Some carried water buckets. One carried a banjo. Two or three others acted the fool. In Rudd's mind these portrayals reinforced negative stereotypes. What needed to be remembered he said, was the "few old Colored soldiers, members of the Grand Army of the Republic, who marched with soldierly bearing with the others." Moved by this same scene he went on to say, "It was an inspiration to see those men, who had faced the foe in the thick of the fight, show that they were still ready and willing to do battle for the flag that made us free."[3]

In his campaign to defend the dignity of African Americans, Rudd challenged Catholics as well as Protestants. Though he insisted Catholics in the church would receive black members as brothers and sisters, at times the editor had to confront bigoted members of the church who sought to insult African Americans. On one occasion, Rudd took aim at the editor of the *Adam*. Given the moral proclivities of the race, the newspaper claimed, it did little good to teach black citizens the doctrines of Catholicism. Rudd responded sharply and insisted black converts make as good a Christian as whites.

Rudd's defense of the dignity of the race was bolstered by his decision to regularly feature accomplished African Americans in the pages of his newspaper. As mentioned earlier, Rudd was an admirer of Fr. Augustus Tolton, the first black priest ordained in the United States to openly disclose his racial heritage. Rudd followed the ministry of this church leader in the pages of the *ACT*. On one occasion, Rudd printed a letter penned by his newspaper partner James T. Whitson in which Whitson described the honor directed toward the black priest while the two were on a visit to Quincy, Illinois. Whitson claimed, "Even the little boys and girls as do also the adults, raise their hats to him as he passes along the streets and the good pious white Catholics are as ready to kneel down and receive a blessing at his hands as the whitest man on whom the sun ever shone."[4] Rudd highlighted other successful Catholics as well. Among them was William S. Lofton, a graduate of the dentistry program at

Howard University and an important leader in the Colored Catholic Congress movement. Similarly Rudd introduced his readers to James Armstrong, a respected lay Catholic leader from Chicago, who would prove to be an important ally in Tolton's work in the Windy City.

In his campaign to silence white critics of the race while at the same time trying to bolster racial pride in his black readers, Rudd sometimes featured successful women of color in the pages of the *ACT*. Rudd printed the obituary of Mary Frances Augustine, one of Philadelphia's most accomplished caterers and the mother of an important Colored Catholic Congress leader, Jerome P. Augustine. Another woman of color featured in the *ACT* was Cincinnati native Miss Ida Gray who had been elected vice president of her dental class in Ann Arbor, Michigan. Rudd's decision to highlight these women who were assuming nontraditional roles outside of the home yields some insight as to his views on the rights of women.

Rudd's promotion of the dignity of African Americans is also evidenced by his desire to see monuments erected in honor of important black history makers. On one occasion he expressed his displeasure with a group of black leaders who were contemplating the erection of a monument to one of the nation's white statesmen. Condemning their shortsightedness he wrote, "Are there no Colored men among the living or the dead who were contemporaries and coworkers with these great men in the struggle for liberty? Are we to forever extol the praises of the white man and find nothing in the Negro courage, virtue, character and devotion worthy of monument?"[5] Rudd subsequently praised the work of Lewis Hayden, a black abolitionist who had initiated a campaign to raise a monument in honor of Crispus Attucks. Attucks was a black patriot believed to have been the first to die in America's campaign for independence. Commenting on Hayden's initiative Rudd wrote, "It appears the Colored people are awaking to the importance of erecting monuments to commemorate the memory of their heroic dead. They have very wisely started off by erecting one to the memory of Chrispus [sic] Attucks, who struck the first authentic blow for independence in America."[6]

As a rationale to justify their bigotry, critics of the race often pointed to the backward condition of African Americans residing in the South. At the time of the *ACT*'s publication, most black citizens still resided south of the Mason Dixon Line. As white community leaders agitated for the segregation of the races throughout the country, it appears the criticism of southern blacks escalated. One consistent charge leveled against the former bondsmen was that they were regressing. Rudd and other African American leaders of the era felt it necessary to counter this narrative and set the record straight.

In 1891 the editor of the *ACT* decided to join forces with two other newspapers—the *Plaindealer* of Detroit and Ida B. Wells-Barnett's *Memphis Free Speech*. This was done in an effort to discover the true condition of African Americans living in the states formerly allied with the Confederacy. The three newspapers pooled resources to hire a correspondent to travel the country in order to gather information. Discrediting the critics of the race, Rudd later wrote, "The letters and correspondents [sic] will certainly prove highly interesting, to those, who are interested in the development of the race. It is sheer nonsense to talk about the Colored people going backward; they are doing no such thing."[7] In the summer of 1891, Rudd published a report from Sarah Cole, an African American schoolteacher from Cincinnati. She also detailed the progress the former bondsmen were making. Some were involved in business ventures; others were pursing educational opportunities. Subsequently Ed Reed, who was on Rudd's payroll for a time, was sent to make a sweep across the South. He too wrote in to highlight the progress being made by black southerners. Reed was fortunate to return home; he was very nearly lynched by a group of white men near Water Valley, Mississippi.

Voting Rights

Rudd's advocacy for racial justice and the cause of equality required him to draw attention to several pressing issues of concern to African Americans. He took aim at the legislature of Mississippi's decision in 1890 to force a new constitution on its citizenry, effectively disenfranchising its black residents. In response to the legislature's decision, Rudd printed a pointed exchange condemning the action.

> It does "pass comprehension" that in the midst of this nineteenth century Which is so boastful of its "open bibles," of its liberty of conscience, of its public and Sunday schools, of its preached Gospel, of its beneficent and charitable works, that there could be found a body of legislators that would dare to place such a provision in a State Constitution, and further, would make that Constitution binding upon the people without submitting it to their approval or vote. Either the people of Mississippi have become heathen or worse, or else enslaved by a set of satanic infidels. Such is the only explanation we can give.[8]

Rudd also took up his pen to further condemn this injustice: "The same old Satan that enslaved and still oppresses a part of the people of Mississippi, kept them in ignorance and still terrorizes the weak and defenseless of that commonwealth, reaches up his unholy hand through the New Mississippi Constitution, to destroy the warming rays of charity which seek in material bequests to aid the development of religion in that beautiful, yet suffering and benighted State."[9]

Tellingly, Rudd linked Satan's unholy work with the disenfranchisement of black voters.

Public Accommodations

With the worsening racial climate in the last decade of the nineteenth century, black citizens found themselves being denied equal access to restaurants, hotels, and other public accommodations. At the same time, public and political support for federal mandates protecting the rights of African Americans began to wane. In 1883 the Civil Rights Act that had been initially passed in 1875 was ruled unconstitutional. People of color were now at the mercy of state legislatures. In the north the voiding of the Civil Rights Act resulted in the passage of new state legislation drafted to protect black citizens. But even these legislative mandates were routinely underenforced. Moreover, penalties for violating discrimination laws were often inconsequential.

As discriminatory laws against persons of color took hold in sections of the South, it appears that some bigoted entrepreneurs doing business in Cincinnati felt emboldened. Instances of racial discrimination in the city led Rudd in January of 1890 to speak out against offending business owners. Cincinnati was being "outraged" by the practice of this type of unlawful discrimination, he explained. He continued, "When the best known and ablest Colored men can be insulted by anyone who sees fit to do so and no one speaks in resentment then it is time to ask, what is the Negro good for?" He further warned,

We have rested under this thing long enough and shall no longer be silent. . . .We know this will strike hard. But we are prepared to give and receive hard blows. This country is not properly civilized and will not be until men learn to treat each other on their merits and not the color of their skin, their eyes, or their hair.[10]

In the *ACT* Rudd sometimes published the names of businesses guilty of refusing equitable service to black residents. For example, Rudd drew attention to a sign in John Heider's West Fifth Street eatery letting black customers know they would need to eat in the rear of the restaurant. Rudd questioned whether or not it was appropriate for African Americans to patronize such establishments. On another occasion he published a letter in the *ACT* informing the readers that a local amusement park (Coney Island) was refusing African Americans entrance. This same letter bemoaned the fact that the denial of service on the basis of race seemed to be getting more common. The contributor further urged Cincinnati's African Americans to take action against these establishments.

In the fall of 1891, Rudd challenged business owners guilty of breaking the state's antidiscrimination laws. He called for the arrest of the offending barbers, restaurant owners, and theatrical managers. "It is a crime against the laws of Ohio that is punishable by fine and imprisonment; Brand a few of the criminals with [the] States hot iron and the foolishness will stop. Let the law be enforced or repealed," he urged.[11] Such rhetoric must have placed the editor of the *ACT* in some danger. Still he courageously persisted.

On some occasions Rudd's advocacy for the fair treatment of members of the race was couched in less hostile rhetoric. Rudd drew attention to the economic cost of discrimination. He suggested that because African Americans were being treated unjustly many were not visiting the Queen City, and as much as 1.5 million dollars in economic benefit had been lost to the city as a result of it being passed up as a site for major conventions.

In the spring of 1890, Rudd's campaign against racial discrimination in public accommodations moved from mere rhetoric to direct legal action. When visiting Cincinnati's P. C. Butler Delicatessen with two of his newspaper's advertisers, the proprietor refused to serve Rudd. Rudd and his two associates were offended by the insult. The editor of the *ACT* subsequently felt it his duty to take legal action against the eatery. He contacted the attorney J. R. Foraker who filed suit against the restaurant on the basis of the discriminatory action. The courts ruled in favor of Rudd; he was subsequently awarded a one hundred dollar judgment. Rudd later commented on the ruling: "The putrescent sore of United States prejudice, is a cancerous growth and should be speedily removed."[12]

Rudd's campaign against discrimination in public accommodations also led him to object to a local doctor, Dr. Judkins, when he proposed housing black and white patients separately. Rudd claimed such a proposal was put forward to serve the doctor's prejudice rather than the public good. He further concluded the action was shameful and in need of being immediately remedied.

Separate Coach Legislation

Rudd strongly opposed the separate coach legislation enacted throughout the country in the last decades of the nineteenth century. He believed such laws were demeaning to African Americans. The editor's campaign for racial justice compelled him to speak out against these discriminatory laws meant to force people of color into racially segregated train cars.

The first separate coach law was passed in Tennessee in 1881; its passage predated the establishment of the *ACT*. Other states began enacting similar legislation after Rudd began publishing his newspaper. Florida passed a version of this restrictive code in 1887; Mississippi in 1888; Texas in 1889; Louisiana in 1890; and Alabama, Georgia, and Arkansas in 1891. The legality of forcing black citizens into separate train cars was eventually challenged in the US Supreme Court. Advocates for racial integration lost when the Plessy vs. Ferguson decision was handed down in 1896. This same notorious ruling served as the foundation for Jim Crow.

As early as 1887, Rudd had begun speaking out against separate coach laws. He had occasion in the years following to voice his opposition to the practice as state after state followed suit. In 1890 several states considered various versions of this discriminatory legislation. When Tennessee passed a second separate coach law in 1891, Rudd wrote, "The State of Tennessee, has disgraced herself in the recent legislation . . . discriminating against a large and intelligent portion of her citizens. How long such outrageous proceedings will continue, God alone knows. Some time or other people will learn common sense."[13]

Rudd's anger over separate coach legislation could not be contained when Kentucky, the state of his birth, passed in 1892 a law segregating train cars. Up to the time of its passage, Rudd had confidently asserted that wiser heads in the legislature would prevail. Rudd's faith in his fellow Kentuckians, however, proved misplaced. After the law was approved, Rudd's frustration boiled over. He wrote, "Men of Kentucky, this is criminal. Who can tell how many of these latter day saints sucked their infantile nourishment from black paps?

The white men of Kentucky have robbed the Negro race of its identity, and now that they have done so wish to hide the crime drawing an artificial line. The separate coach law is an outrage. How long O Lord, how long?"[14]

Speaking to this same issue Rudd wrote, "The Kentucky legislature has covered itself with infamy. A governing body 'contemptible' enough to pass this legislation should be 'kicked boots and body from the State it infests,'" Rudd insisted. He went on to declare the odious law a "disgrace" to nineteenth century civilization and a violation of the "spirit and genius" of the nineteenth century, the Declaration of Independence, and the Constitution.[15] After reporting on the legislature's action, Rudd was forced to concede, "American popular opinion is rotten in many places, especially when justice to the Negro citizen is concerned. We must 'cry aloud and spare not.'" Finally, in the same publication he wrote, "the river of oppression is brimming full."[16]

Emigration

Rudd believed in the full equality of African Americans. He was convinced the country's former bondsmen had earned the right to enjoy the fruits of the republic they had helped to build. Any suggestion this much-abused people might need to emigrate from this country offended his sense of fairness. It made little difference to Rudd whether the initiative originated with whites or members of the black community. Rudd did not show any patience toward African Americans who wanted to leave the United States because they believed their full equality would never be recognized. In his heart the editor was an optimist who had faith America could yet live up to the noble ideals expressed in the founding documents of the republic.

In the winter of 1888, after some in the African American community proposed the creation of a colony in South America, Rudd had occasion to address the issue of emigration. The editor's views on the matter come through clearly. He wrote, "The American Negro has felled the forests and moulded [sic] the bricks in all the Southland, he is part and parcel of America's greatness. Any one who thinks that he is fool enough now to leave the monuments of his unrequited toil must be sadly deluded. This talk of exodus makes us tired. The only exodus the American Negro needs is to exodus himself out of bed in the early morning, and save the money he earns. His other ills will disappear by this and the practice of virtue, quicker than any other way."[17]

In an editorial published in the September 28, 1889, edition of the *ACT*, the editor again took up the question of black emigration from the South.

> We have read with much concern the expressions of men concerning the colonization of a very large part of the Southern people. We must face facts first then speculate afterwards. These people who have acquired lands and established business[es] [they] will not give up without a struggle, they are a part of the South. To them the South justly belongs. If the black race were requited for their toil there for the last century and a half it would own every foot of soil from the Delaware to the Rio Grande. Every Forest and field has felt the effect of the Negro's brawn, and almost every old family of all the races there have eaten the bread at the labor of the Negroes hand. He loves his native soil, and nothing short of a bloody revolution will make many leave the land of their birth for new and untried fields. Thank God this is so. We may suffer yet a while, but the justice of the Almighty will prevail at last. The Negro will not go.[18]

Immigration

Rudd showed concern for immigrants coming into the country in order to make a new start. His empathy for these aspiring citizens set him apart from many African Americans who resented the fact that they were forced to compete with newcomers for low-wage jobs. Despite competing economic interests, Rudd urged members of the black community not to discriminate against this vulnerable group. He wrote, "The Colored race cannot afford to entertain prejudice toward foreign born Americans, because their customs and habits may not conform to native born Americans. It is . . . sensible for the race to cultivate their sympathy and love."[19] Rudd's position as a Catholic also may help explain his distaste for the American Protective Association (APA), a secret society harboring an anti-Catholic and anti-immigrant animus. The editor took pleasure in knowing so few African Americans were members of the APA. In his mind it was simply not possible for one to be loyal both to the oath of this anti-immigrant organization and to the US Constitution.

Though Rudd supported immigration, he was in sympathy with Catholics who believed those coming into the United States needed to assimilate. The editor's desire to see recent arrivals melded into the fabric of American culture was likely influenced by the marginalization he as a black man and Catholic often felt. Rudd imagined a national community where no group would be forced to the margins. In such a community, distinctions of language and culture would necessarily be played down for the sake of the unity of the whole.

Rudd's support of this accommodationist position, however, is not easy to reconcile with his warm relations with the German Catholic Central Verein and other like-minded, more nationalistic Catholics who were less comfortable with American institutions and culture. Nevertheless Rudd's advocacy for assimilation appears to have been largely free from the xenophobia and ethnic prejudice present in others calling for the assimilation of immigrants.

CHAPTER SIX

Campaigning for Equality and Racial Justice

Rudd's program to promote justice and equality for African Americans took a number of forms. Because he believed the path of racial uplift passed through the door of economic opportunity, the editor of the *American Catholic Tribune* pressed for a level playing field for black professionals and laborers. Rudd further decried instances of violence against black citizens deprived of the due process of the law even as he promoted racial integration.

Economic Opportunities

Critical to Rudd's campaign for racial equality was his desire to see avenues of economic opportunity opened for African Americans. During the time Rudd published the *ACT*, black citizens routinely found themselves blocked from well-paying, skilled jobs. Systemic racism stood as a formidable impediment to economic equality. African Americans from all parts of the country persevered, pushing back and succeeding in every field of endeavor. Yet when all was said and done, far too many could find work only in physically demanding jobs in agriculture, fishing, and mining.[1] Throughout his years as the editor of the *ACT*, Rudd worked to draw attention to these inequities. But his efforts did not stop with his editorials. Rudd's printing operation provided jobs and skilled training for people of color seeking employment.

Rudd's campaign to secure jobs for African Americans was in part conditioned by his own observations in and around Cincinnati. There were no members of the black community employed as streetcar drivers, motormen, or conductors. He also bemoaned the fact that only one black schoolteacher had been employed legally in the city. Rudd further took aim at the practice of denying African Americans the right to serve as firefighters.

Rudd took special interest in the employment of African American teachers, but by the end of the 1880s the black teaching profession in Cincinnati was in jeopardy. The school board proved unwilling to place black instructors in integrated schools. Unhappy with the board's position on the matter, in the spring of 1890 Rudd took the extraordinary step of going in person to speak to W. H. Morgan, the superintendent of Cincinnati's schools. He hoped to convince the administrator to hire black teachers. The encounter was not a pleasant one. Morgan, with the air of an "autocrat" and the dignity of a "numskull," refused to hire black teachers to teach white students, Rudd reported. The editor further complained he himself was insulted. Comparing Morgan to the former superintendent, E. E. White, Rudd called Morgan an "intellectual pigmy." Rudd explained that in the meeting the superintendent claimed to be a "good Republican." He wrote, "We [do] not care a fig whether he be a Democrat, Republican, Prohibitionist, Greenbacker, or

Mugwump: we want simple justice. Neither prejudice nor bighead will stop the onward sweep of the great wave of honest public opinion."[2]

Though Rudd fought against those who refused to hire qualified African Americans, he nonetheless counseled members of the race to take matters into their own hands. By founding black-owned businesses, Rudd believed members of the African American community could make progress in improving their economic standing in society. Encouraging more than empty political discourse, Rudd on one occasion wrote, "One business firm is worth more to a community, than a thousand politicians."[3] He declared, "Do you want employment for yourselves and your children? Make it."[4] In essence Rudd was encouraging African Americans with financial resources to follow his lead, to do as he had done with his own printing enterprise. On the topic of job creation, the editor offered the following advice: "If Colored men wish their sons and daughters to occupy important positions in life, those of us who have money must launch into business. We must commence if necessary on a small scale and aim to increase our stock and trade as our means and opportunities afford. We must learn to do business with all classes of people. As the demands of our business require more help let us employ Colored men and women or employ some Colored and some white and in this way set the example for our white brethren."[5]

Rudd believed the city of Cincinnati to be a good place for African Americans to open businesses. He imagined that these start-ups would be patronized by both white and black customers. There was room in the city for a mercantile store, a dry goods establishment, and perhaps a shoe factory, he contended. Rudd in turn praised the efforts of black entrepreneurs who took on the challenge of starting businesses.

In pursuit of the equality of economic opportunity, Rudd recognized the value of collective bargaining. During the latter decades of the nineteenth century many laborers, including Catholics, were entering trade unions to protest poor working conditions and to agitate for higher wages. The head of the American church, James Cardinal Gibbons, had encouraged Pope Leo XIII not to condemn membership in labor organizations. But Rudd's support of organized labor was conflicted. He believed economic prosperity was being hindered among African Americans in part because of the refusal of labor union leaders to allow members of the black community to join. Rudd, however, did not believe members of the race should passively sit by waiting for white union leaders to take the initiative. He suggested black workers needed to act on their own behalf by organizing to protect their economic interests.

In his campaign to promote economic fairness, Rudd was quick to condemn the crop mortgage system of the South. From the early days of the *ACT,* articles denouncing the type of tenant farming practiced in states formally allied with the Confederacy could be found. Rudd believed this contract system was exploitive. White landowners often further impoverished vulnerable farmers (many of whom were black) by paying their tenants with paper slips redeemable only at the plantation store, which often charged exorbitant prices for staple goods. Over time, laborers essentially became bound to their employer by the accumulation of the mounting debt ballooning season after season.

Rudd's views on economics and justice moved beyond simply promoting the interests of African Americans. He sought the establishment of a more equitable economic order—one in which the standard of living for all elements of society would be improved. But during the years of the publication of the *ACT,* the interests of labor and capital were often at odds. Sometimes these conflicts became violent. This was the case both in the Haymarket Riot of 1886 and the Homestead Strike of 1892. As a Catholic, Rudd looked to the church for answers. For him these two classes were members of one family under God, and he applied his belief in the "Fatherhood of God and Brotherhood of Man" to the chasm dividing the "haves" from the "have nots."

When Pope Leo XIII in 1891 issued *Rerum Novarum,* an encyclical addressing many of the social problems created by industrialization, Rudd enthusiastically endorsed it. He even chose to serialize the teaching letter and print it in its entirety in the *ACT.* There was much in this foundational document of Catholic social teaching to be embraced: the dignity of all members of the human family, the role of the church in addressing the needs of society, the encouragement of a familial spirit between capital and labor, and the church's advocacy on behalf of society's most vulnerable members. Rudd also appreciated the pope's rejection of socialism even as the head of the Catholic Church pointed out flaws in an unrestrained capitalist economy. Finally, the document supported a more humane capitalistic system—one that recognized the right of labor groups to organize and even to strike if circumstances required such action.

Social Catholicism was coming of age at the same time Rudd was establishing the *ACT.* Over time this movement recognized benevolence and charity were not all that was required of Christians seeking to live piously. Instead the teachings of Christianity needed to be applied to the structural inequities disadvantaging society's most-at-risk populations. Those promoting Social Catholicism, including Rudd, sought to mine the church's theological tradition in the hopes of establishing a more just social order. In the process unchecked capitalism fell under ethical scrutiny.

What became clear to many was that unrestrained market forces created victims. Those most at risk were women, children, the poor, and diverse people groups.

Rudd's faith in the Catholic Church's power to rightly order society places him in close proximity to a group often overlooked in historical studies of the period: proponents of the black Social Gospel. According to Gary Dorrien, this group was comprised of African American church leaders who sought to transform society into a more just social order. Proponents of the Social Gospel believed that Christian teaching could be effectively applied to society's structural inequities. Some of these same enthusiasts believed the kingdom of God would subsequently be initiated on earth as a result of this work. For black proponents, the Social Gospel's stand against racial discrimination was the most important societal injustice in need of addressing. In his study Dorrien identifies a number of key leaders of the black Social Gospel movement. Among them are Ida B. Wells-Barnett, T. Thomas Fortune, and Thomas Wyatt Turner, all contemporaries of Rudd. Rudd corresponded and worked closely with this group of journalists and activists even though his Catholic faith set him apart theologically. Though the editor's Catholic faith was likely the reason he is passed over in Dorrien's study, in many respects Rudd's work resembles that of the black Social Gospellers.[6]

Like other African American proponents of the Social Gospel, Rudd sought to see Christian teachings applied to the institutional structures impeding the progress of the race. But with Rudd the Social Gospel message was grounded in the embrace of the Catholic Church's uplifting work across the centuries rather than in Protestant theology and eschatology. To be clear, Rudd did not hold a postmillennial eschatology. Nor did he believe God's kingdom would be established on earth prior to the eschaton. But Rudd did look forward to the establishment of what he called a "New Civilization," one in which the equality of African Americans would be realized. The basis of this civilization was to be Christianity—authentic Catholic Christianity. This new civilization, Rudd claimed, would embrace "all that is charitable in social intercourse, fair in diplomatic relations and commercial exchange, and beautiful and pure in art and music, elegant and Christianly in literature and pleasing to God—our Creator above all things, our neighbor as ourselves."[7] Rudd's Christian critique of society closely resembled Protestant criticisms. In other ways, however, Rudd's message was polemical; it clearly imagined the Catholic Church to be on the vanguard of social renewal.

The Campaign against Mob Violence and the Practice of Lynching

Daniel Rudd joined other leading African American activists, including the outspoken Ida B. Wells-Barnett, in the fight against mob violence and the brutal practice of lynching. Evidence from the *ACT* suggests Rudd's thinking developed over time on this important justice issue. Early in the life of the *ACT,* the editor simply reported the executions of black men without much commentary. But as the years passed he became increasingly more direct in his condemnation of the practice. In 1889 Rudd responded to an article that appeared in the *Catholic Universe* of Cleveland. The author claimed that though he held a kind feeling for blacks, he nonetheless believed African American communities needed to be ruled by Caucasians. He further was convinced of the need to practice what he euphemistically labeled "natural law," particularly in locales where black residents outnumbered whites.

Rudd strongly objected to his coreligionist's position, labeling the article a "bit of nonsense." Such a stand ran the risk of keeping breath in what Rudd called the "most horrid spectre [sic] of the present century." The editor of the *ACT* further asked what the contributor meant by "natural law." In response to the column Rudd continued, "Are we to understand that the hundreds of thousands of Negroes who have been murdered for doing what the law, in its plainest terms, says they have the right to do were murdered according to 'natural law'? Is the unmerciful beating of innocent and helpless women and children in the still midnight hours, by masked and bloodthirsty scoundrels a part of that 'natural law?' Is the burning of the hard earned homes and chasing of trembling and unarmed men with rifles and shot guns, a part of that 'natural law?' " Defending the race, Rudd pointed to the poor example whites had set for African Americans. It was Caucasians who taught black offenders such crimes, Rudd claimed. African Americans also enjoyed a higher literacy rate than did the white population, the editor pointed out.[8]

With regard to his thinking on the cruel practice of lynching, evidence from the *ACT* indicates that 1892 was a watershed year for Rudd. The editor, like other African Americans around the country, was horrified to learn the details of the lynchings of Thomas Moss, Calvin McDowell, and Will Stewart that occurred on the evening of March 9, 1892. The mob murder of these three Memphis residents, who had no criminal records, seems to have pushed the issue of lynching to the top of Rudd's program for justice.

In Cincinnati as in other locales across the country, the black community followed the news in Memphis with dismay, denouncing the lynchings as a gross miscarriage of justice. Subsequently Rudd joined other black city leaders in a mass meeting held to denounce the murders. The assembly not only condemned the lynchings but also expressed the community's "deep distress" and "heartfelt sympathies" for the grieving survivors. A circular setting aside May 31 as a day of fasting and prayer was produced at the assembly. The resolution further called for agitation in the press. After African American well-wishers attempted unsuccessfully to persuade one of the city's white-owned newspapers to publish the resolution, Daniel Rudd stepped forward to offer his support. A report detailing the editor's contribution to the cause was reproduced in the *ACT*:

> Though we are oppressed, starved and slain, yet we thank God that he has enabled us to own a paper among our race that will, and can plead the cause of our people. For when the white papers of Cincinnati refused to publish our sentiments Mr. Dan A. Rudd, editor and proprietor of the American Catholic Tribune stepped forward and said, "Gentlemen, I am a poor man, but I love my race. Give me your rejected manuscript and I will publish it and donate and mail five hundred copies free of charge to any person to whom you may want them sent."[9]

Throughout 1892 Rudd continued the fight against lynching from his base of operation in Cincinnati. He took a leading role in organizing a national convention to protest the unjust practice. The two-day assembly was held in the Queen City beginning on July 4. Despite a lower than expected attendance the organizers pressed on. In an article published in the *ACT*, Rudd insisted the practice of mob law surpassed other dangers confronting the country including the threat posed by "giant trusts and corporations." He wrote:

> Whatever danger may lurk in these, it is not so imminent as the mob law that terrorizes the people by wholesale murders so brutal and shocking in their nature as to raise doubt in the minds of some, of the civilization of the American people. This thing cannot last. Justice must some-

where find the point of retribution. The United States Government can call out the army and navy to save the life of a few seals, or to resent some insult offered to a drunken sailor in the most remote corner of the earth, yet when men and women, citizens of the United States are hung, shot, skinned alive or burned at the stake all over the country, for crimes of which they have never been proven guilty, this mighty government whose vigilance bids the greatest nations quake, declares she cannot protect her citizens at home. . . . If bad example continues to prevail, it will have a very serious effect on the whole people and sooner or later inevitable dissolution, anarchy and consequent desolation will prevail. How long, O Lord, how long?[10]

Racial Integration

Even as a resident of Ohio, a northern state, Rudd still witnessed instances of racial discrimination on a regular basis. School systems from across the state were often the offending parties. Throughout his publishing career, Rudd championed the cause of school integration. Opposition to Rudd's efforts came not only from Caucasians, but also from the African American community. Some in this latter group believed the existence of race schools insured the employment of black teachers. This was the editorial position of the influential newspaper the *Christian Recorder,* a weekly published by the African Methodist Episcopal Church. Other black leaders supported segregated schools because they believed that the prejudice of white teachers adversely impacted black students. Moreover, proponents of black schools wanted to see African American role models teaching in classrooms where students of color were in attendance.

Rudd and his allies in the cause of racial desegregation had much to celebrate after the Ohio legislature passed the

Ely-Arnett Bill early in 1887. This important legislation not only dismantled Ohio's black laws, but it also laid the legal groundwork for the desegregation of the state's schools. After Rudd received the news of the historic legislation's passage he exulted, "A Cry for Justice is Heard." He continued to oppose racially segregated schools after the dismantling of the state's black laws. Sometimes he employed graphic language in the cause. On one occasion he wrote, "Like a slimy thing the pernicious system of separate schools has wound itself into our very existence and it seems impossible to completely eradicate it."[11]

In the months following the passage of the Ely-Arnett Bill, Rudd promoted both the cause of racial integration and the campaign to encourage the hiring of black teachers. In August of 1887, Rudd drew attention to Charles W. Bell's appointment to a local teaching post. He labeled the hire a "triumph" and "first grand step in the march of progress." He referred to Bell as a "gentleman every inch" and a "master of his art." Rudd believed the advocacy that had led to Bell's appointment might have also resulted in the defeat of segregated schools had the effort been commenced earlier.[12]

Rudd's opposition to segregated schools placed him in conflict with leaders of Ohio's black educational institutions. When some advocates of the state's black colleges sought to have their institutions receive a portion of the public funds previously earmarked to go to the Ohio State University, Rudd objected. He believed such action threatened to nullify portions of the Ely-Arnett Bill and was, therefore, illegal. If such a measure were to be passed, Rudd warned, it would not be long before the Ohio State University closed its doors to black students altogether. In the *ACT*, Rudd commented on Wilberforce University's support for the proposal to funnel funds to select black institutions across the state. In response Rudd claimed the move would make it possible for any black educational institution, regardless of the school's quality, to demand its share of the designated funds.[13]

The passage of the Ely-Arnett Bill and the subsequent closing of some of Cincinnati's black schools did not yield the results Rudd had anticipated. As it turned out, city school administrators were reluctant to hire black teachers to fill positions in its integrated schools. Stung by the injustice, Rudd posed the following question in the *ACT*: "What right has the state to draw taxes from all the people for school general purposes and then to discriminate against any class of citizens?" He further proposed an injunction to stop payment for what he termed "illegal schools." In the pages of the *ACT*, Rudd reported on an effort to address the superintendent's refusal to hire black teachers. The "exclusion of the Cincinnati colored teachers," he argued, "was the result of prejudice and could not be justified upon any principle of fair play."[14]

In the fall of 1889, under the heading "Justice Reigns," Rudd reported on a mean-spirited initiative contrived by the administrators of the community schools of Felicity. The editor accused these school officials of seeking to divide the student body along racial lines. When their underhanded aims failed, the school moved under a false pretense to close its doors. In the process a number of teachers of color lost their income. Rudd informed his readers how one of the teachers, A. G. Hubbard, successfully recovered his lost wages through the court system. In this same story the editor reported with some satisfaction that others were following Hubbard's example.[15]

Rudd's confidence in school administrators from across the state reveals a naivety on his part. Given the racial prejudice against African Americans, it is hard to see how he could have retained confidence in the good faith of school officials, beholden as they were to the parents of white school children. Even as incidents of discrimination escalated through the last decades of the nineteenth century, Rudd seemed to remain stubbornly confident both in the collective political power of African American voters and in the state's court system. He once confidently contended that should African American teachers be fired as a result of the desegregation of Cincinnati's schools, black activists would "guard with jealous care the interests of the race and dispute at every point the march of un American prejudice."[16] In the end, however, black teachers lost their jobs as a result of school integration in Ohio.

But a glimmer of hope radiated from his beloved faith community. Rudd could point to initiatives in the Catholic Church—programs propelled by a force that seemed to run counter to the bigotry in society. Many charitable programs were initiated to reach out to African Americans. Among the institutions providing services were schools, hospitals, and orphanages. Rudd could call attention to the willingness on the part of the church to ordain black catechists and priests, but he also had to contend with the fact that the church was peopled by members infected with the same racial prejudice so pervasive in nineteenth-century American society.

As a member of the African American community, Rudd spoke out when other black citizens were denied opportunities as a result of racial discrimination. But as a Catholic, Rudd sometimes witnessed what he believed to be the unfair treatment of his fellow religionists. He also contended for the rights of women and people of color living beyond the borders of the United States. His cry for justice was a cry that reached beyond matters of racial equity.

CHAPTER SEVEN

Matters of Justice for Catholics beyond Concerns of Race

Rudd's moral compass led him to oppose injustices beyond race concerns. Another important aspect of Rudd's work was his advocacy on behalf of fellow Catholics. At a time when most of the citizens of the United States claimed a Protestant religious heritage, Catholics found their interests sometimes threatened. Many Protestants were hostile to the Catholic faith, believing the pope to be the antichrist and the church's hierarchal structure to be inimical to the spirit of American democracy. Though this country's history of discrimination against Catholics goes back to the colonial era, its most ugly manifestation peaked through the middle decades of the nineteenth century. In the decade Rudd was born, political nativism reached its zenith in urban centers along the East Coast, including in Boston and New York. During the worst outbreaks of anti-Catholic sentiment, religious violence escalated, and churches and convents were burned.

Public School Education

In his quest to see Catholics treated as equal citizens of the republic, Rudd staked out a position on the education of Catholic youth very much in line with his coreligionists. While Rudd was getting his publishing career underway in Springfield, Ohio, Catholic church leaders in the United States were calling for Catholics to educate their children in Catholic institutions. Influential clergymen had long objected to the "nonsectarian" form of religion being promoted in the nation's public schools. They believed the watered-down, least common denominator sort of Christian faith encouraged in public schools was simply not substantial enough to stave off the forces threatening the nation's youth, threats like materialism and formal unbelief. Catholic church leaders also objected to the classroom use of the King James Bible as well as Protestant versions of both the Sermon on the Mount and the Ten Commandments. This critical view of the American public school system was not shared by many Protestants. Nor would many public school administrators admit any inherent, denominational bias in the Christian-based, moral training encouraged in the nation's public schools.

Like many other coreligionists of his era Rudd thought it unfair to tax Catholics in order to fund America's public schools—institutions they could not in good conscience use. Rudd further believed Catholics could not be blamed for refusing to send their children to public school in part because he viewed these same institutions as centers for Protestant proselytizing. Forcing Catholics to pay for schools they could not use, then burdening the same population with the expense of a religious education, amounted to a double taxation. Rudd and many of his Catholic counterparts believed education to be a matter in which parental rights took precedent over the state.

Rudd was a strong believer in the importance of training the heart and not just the intellect. He believed it to be impossible to teach morality apart from the principles of the Christian faith. On one occasion Rudd wrote, "If this Republic is to stand, [its] children must have a good, practical, moral education, that is given hand in hand with the physical and intellectual. To teach correct morals entirely outside of the principals [sic] of Christianity, is impossible. Therefore children should have a Christian Education."[1] Rudd further believed that if society would commit to following the model of education being promoted by the Catholic Church there would be no reason in the future to fret over how the nation's children would turn out.

Predictably, Rudd opposed the idea of removing God or religion from the classroom. In one instance he printed an exchange detailing a list of societal ills that were believed to have resulted from such an exclusion. Among these social blights were the rising divorce rate, an increase in the number of cases of insanity and suicide, and a spike in immorality.

Like his fellow Catholics, Rudd objected to attempts by local school boards to oversee the administration of Catholic educational institutions. In April 1888 he gave voice to his opposition to such an effort proposed by a governing body in Massachusetts. He wrote:

> The State has under consideration the enactment of a law, which will grant the State [the] right to inspect the parochial schools. This the Catholics oppose, unless the State agrees to divide the school funds. This our Protestant friends are unwilling to do. The whole fact of the matter is, that it is the beginning of an attempt of our Protestant friends, to check the rapid growth of the parochial schools

in America. Massachusetts is taking the lead in this respect, and if she succeeds, her example will be followed in other states. Protestantism and Catholicity are like oil and water, they wont mix; therefore it stands Catholics in hand to fight to the bitter end for non interference.[2]

Rudd's Catholic viewpoint on education policy did not mean he agreed with his coreligionists in all points. For example, Rudd criticized members of the Catholic Church for discriminating against black students seeking to enter Catholic schools. He also differed from most Catholics on public school policy in that he supported the Blair Federal Aid to Education Bill drafted by Senate Republican Henry W. Blair of New Hampshire. This legislation was widely supported by people of color in the United States because it not only protected the rights of black citizens but also proposed measures to improve the nation's schools, especially in the South. Rudd saw merit in the federal government's involvement in the improvement of schools. This oversight was especially needed in southern states where most African Americans were educated. In a meeting of the Afro-American Press Association held in Louisville in 1887, Rudd urged the passage of the bill. Catholics generally did not support the legislation because they believed education needed to remain a local issue. Moreover, some Catholics found Henry Blair's anti-Catholic sentiments, occasionally aired from the floor of the Senate, offensive.[3]

Home Rule for Ireland

A read through the editorials of the *ACT* reveals a number of columns devoted to Rudd's support for Ireland's Catholic population living under British colonial rule. Only months before Rudd's creation of the *ACT*, Prime Minister

William E. Gladstone rose in England's House of Commons to present the Government of Ireland Bill, which would come to be known by many as the "First Home Rule Bill." This important legislation proposed the transfer of some governing authority from the British ruling class to moderate representatives of the Catholic Irish nation. Charles Stewart Parnell, the head of what came to be termed the "Home Rule Party," became a leading voice in English politics as an advocate for the rights of Ireland's predominantly Catholic population.

The campaign for autonomy championed by advocates of Irish home rule was widely discussed beyond the borders of the island nation. The drive for self-rule was also a matter of debate in the United States. Many Catholics, including Rudd, believed justice demanded some level of home rule for Ireland's population. Support for Irish home rule extended beyond the walls of the church—advocacy for Irish self-determination was a plank in the Republican platform. Joseph B. Foraker, who served Ohio as governor, and then subsequently represented the state in the US Senate, supported Irish home rule. In a speech he delivered in the spring of 1887, Foraker predicted the country would someday have home rule. Rudd commented on the speech in the *ACT*. If Foraker could convince all of the Republican Party on the matter of home rule, Rudd reasoned it would be an improved political party.

Rudd's support of home rule for Ireland placed him in the company of many prominent non-Catholic, African American leaders who also embraced this cause, including black statesman Frederick Douglass. Because Irish home rule was supported by the Republican Party, it is likely Rudd found many who were willing to sign on to a resolution he proposed at the Afro-American Press Association meeting in 1887. The resolution read: "Whereas, the people of Ireland, like the American Negro, have been suffering and struggling under the injustice of man to man, and Whereas, From every land where an Irishman is found there comes determination unconquerable, and liberal hands to aid in the freedom of the Emerald Isle; therefore, Resolved, That we send hearty greeting and warm congratulations to the sons of Erin for their matchless devotion to a noble cause."[4]

Throughout his years as the proprietor of the *ACT*, Rudd followed events in Ireland. Again in 1891 the editor informed his readers of his concern for the plight of Catholics living under British rule. He wrote rather hyperbolically, "The whole world is interested in struggling, suffering, Ireland, and to the extent of this great sympathy, the people of the earth rejoice in the signs of coming victory for the Irish cause."[5]

Rudd's support for fellow Catholics in Ireland came naturally. As an African American, he understood the stigma of living as a second-class citizen in a country where his race disadvantaged him. The commonalities between the struggles of those seeking Irish independence in Europe and those fighting the oppressive Jim Crow system in the United States were obvious to the editor. He made the connection between the two groups explicit when he wrote, "It hardly seems possible, that civilization would at this point of its development, brook for a moment the scenes that are being enacted in Ireland. . . . But then we do not need to go to Ireland to find cases of injustice. America is full of them as a hill is of ants." In the same article Rudd went on to identify some of the injustices he had in mind: the southern prison system, the crop mortgage system, and the discrimination routinely faced by black travelers in the South.[6]

Evidence of Rudd's advocacy for Ireland's oppressed Catholics is also revealed in a printed exchange published in the *ACT* that condemned the British overlords' cruel treatment of Ireland's renters. Building on this same position, Rudd drew comparisons between the tools used to oust Irish tenants, "writs and crowbar brigades," with the tools employed in the African slave trade, "halters and slave ships." Rudd also saw commonalities between the expulsion of Ireland's citizenry and that of Ida B. Wells-Barnett, who had been previously forced out of her home in Tennessee for speaking against the cruel practice of lynching.[7]

Seizure of Papal Lands

As a champion for justice, Rudd commented on political matters in Italy, especially as they related to the property rights of the pope. The *ACT* condemned the actions of Italian nationalists guilty of seizing papal territories as part of a drive to unite Italy—a campaign that had begun in the middle decades of the nineteenth century. A number of exchanges from other publications condemning the seizures were picked up and subsequently printed by Rudd in the *ACT*. In November of 1888, for example, Rudd published an exchange emphasizing the injustice of such seizures. The contributor explained that the "Vicar of Christ, the Pope" had been "robbed . . . of his temporal dominion and of the [resources] of the Propaganda." The writer of the exchange criticized the "insane Italian revolutionists" for taking by "force and fraud" the "patrimony of the Holy See," making the pontiff little more than "a prisoner in the Vatican."[8] Throughout the life of the *ACT*, Rudd continued to print exchanges decrying the seizure of church land holdings.

In his own editorials Rudd sometimes added his voice to the chorus of Catholics from around the country defending the pope's claims. In the following editorial contribution,

Rudd offered a rationale for why it was necessary for the pontiff to retain his territorial holdings. He wrote:

> The truth is that the head of the Catholic Church should not be the subject of any but the God who created him. He is not free in the exercise of his duties, as spiritual head of the Church, so long as he is in a position to be robbed, insulted and abused by a government that is not only inimical, to the Church but even opposed to every idea of Christianity and revealed religion . . . nothing short of absolute independence will place the Pope in position to carry out his mission, as the vicar of Christ.[9]

On another occasion Rudd took up his pen to address the matter. This time he reminded his readers those who believed the Catholic world had given up on the idea of restoring the temporal power of the pope were deceived. Catholics were indeed aware of the importance of the subject, he continued, and were willing to raise it whenever an appropriate opportunity presented itself.

Rudd's strong defense of the Vatican may have been partially conditioned by Rome's historic support for the African American community in the United States. Rudd and other black Catholics believed they had a trusted ally in the pope. This confidence in the head of the Catholic Church was not without foundation. In 1839 for example, Pope Gregory XVI issued *In Supremo Apostolatus*, a formal proclamation outlawing the slave trade. This document could also be read as a direct condemnation of the institution of slavery as it was then being practiced in the United States. But Rome's concern for people of color in this country did not end with this bold step. In both the Second Plenary Council held in 1866 as well as in the Third Plenary Council held in 1884, Rome pushed American church leaders to minister to the former bondsmen.[10]

The Rights of Women

During the period in which Rudd operated the *ACT*, the rights of women and their role in society were topics of concern. Many traditionalists believed God had ordained women to serve as both wife and mother largely within the confines of the home. From this domestic perch she could dutifully serve her family. Should a young woman want more from life, then the convent was the accepted alternative.

Those espousing what has been labeled the "cult of true womanhood" believed the ideal woman could be characterized by four cardinal virtues: piety, purity, submissiveness, and domesticity. The cult of true womanhood along with the restrictive expectations accompanying this stereotype was broadly embraced by Protestants and Catholics alike. Those who espoused this traditional understanding of a woman's place in society often opposed the efforts of women who sought to break free from these expectations. Women who applied to fill occupations traditionally held by men were often criticized, as were activists who worked for women's suffrage. Many in Rudd's day believed to tamper with the domesticity of the woman was to threaten the stability of civilization and to go against God's will.[11]

One important Catholic writer who promoted a traditional view on the proper position of the woman in society was Fr. Bernard O'Reilly. His popular book *The Mirror of True Womanhood* that was published in 1876 went through seventeen editions up through 1892. O'Reilly believed the woman was the more spiritual of the two sexes. He ascribed to her almost unlimited power either for good or ill. When all was in proper order the sphere of the woman was to be the home. He believed it was in this sanctuary she could be both "queen" and "saint." Therefore it was not advisable for her to trade this place of influence for a public role in society. O'Reilly wrote, "No woman animated by the Spirit of her Baptism . . . ever fancied that she had or could have any other sphere of duty or activity than that home which is her domain, her garden, her paradise, her world."[12]

The leader of the American Catholic Church, Cardinal James Gibbons, wrote about the proper station of the woman in society in his book *Our Christian Heritage*, published in 1889. The woman, he explained, was the "peer of man in origin and destiny, in redemption by the blood of Christ, and in the participation of His spiritual gifts." But though the woman possessed equal rights in society she did not possess what he termed "similar" rights. Following this line of reasoning the churchman attempted to rationalize a more restrictive sphere of influence. The "noblest work given to the woman is to take care of her children," he explained. To restrict the role of the woman to the "gentler vocations" was not to "fetter her aspirations after the higher and better." Rather, he believed that to step outside the bounds of the home might well diminish her honor.[13]

In the Catholic literature of the period addressing the status of women, a Catholic hermeneutic for reading history is discernable. Those holding to the romantic apologetic for Catholicism argued women over the centuries benefited mightily from the church's power to elevate society's most vulnerable members. The primary credit for lifting the woman to her present privileged place was rightly due the Catholic church. Whereas in Greek culture she had been little more than a slave, she now basked in the light of the respect due her. This strong conviction in the church's ameliorating effect on society over the centuries is consistent with Rudd's editorial perspective.[14]

Progressive Catholics challenged the more traditional gender norms being promoted by church leaders including

Gibbons and O'Reilly. Though on at least one occasion
Rudd published an exchange with a more conservative
understanding of the proper place of the woman in society,
he seems rather to have been more sympathetic to those
elements in the church seeking to broaden the woman's
sphere of participation and influence.

Rudd's openness to a more active role for women in the
public sphere is evidenced by his support of journalist, physi-
cian, and activist Mary Britton, a fellow Kentuckian. The
editor printed an extended and provocative paper she delivered to a gathering held in the summer of 1887. He wrote
the following introduction to the controversial article: "Without comment on the terms it proposes we give it to the public for careful perusal."[15] Though Rudd printed the paper, his
introduction is not an enthusiastic endorsement of Britton's
position. It may be that, since he realized that many of his
clerical readers would have been uncomfortable with such a
progressive stand, he was not free to strongly endorse such
a view. Simply printing her paper was likely risky enough.

In her talk Britton apologized for her earlier embrace of
a more traditional position with regard to the role of women
in society. "I now throw away the old ignorant prejudices,
which I am ashamed to have ever held, and stand here this
evening, fearlessly, defending woman suffrage as a potent
agency in public reforms." Though in her address she raised
a number of issues related to gender justice including pay
inequity for women, her primary aim was to secure suffrage.
Once the franchise was won, then all people regardless of
gender would be in the position to pursue his or her own
dreams and aspirations. In their use of scripture, Britton
believed church leaders attempting to subjugate the woman
had "studiously avoided Christ and made much of Paul."
She explained that the reform movement on behalf of the
woman had been initiated by none other than Jesus Christ.

Moreover, she believed granting women the right to vote could be a potent force for good in society. Taxing women without allowing them representation was "tyranny," she claimed.[16] Rudd defended the constitutionality of the woman's right to cast a ballot through his writing in the *ACT*. He also on one occasion praised women for voting in favor of a Catholic cause.

Justice beyond the Borders of the United States

In his pursuit of equity, Rudd kept his eye tuned on instances of injustice occurring around the globe. Being a former slave, he made space in the *ACT* to report on the slave trade in other areas of the world. In one instance the *ACT* reported on the 700,000 individuals being held in bondage in the South American country of Brazil.[17] In another instance he spoke of the reluctance on the part of slaveholders in this same country to free their charges. On another occasion he printed an article detailing the miserable plight of Mexico's agricultural workers laboring in remote reaches of that country.

At least twice the *ACT* reported on the exploitation of people of color living abroad. In one of these instances it was the US government, according to Rudd, that was the culpable party. In May of 1891 Rudd printed an exchange revealing what he believed to be an underhanded plan on the part of the United States to pit the nation of Haiti against what is today the nation of the Dominican Republic. He said this was done for the simple reason of securing a coaling station in the Caribbean for American ships. Rudd responded to the report of this action by writing a strongly worded editorial as direct as any he had published in the *ACT*: "It is the same old story of the white man playing one

Negro against another. . . . The truth is if the white man would keep his finger out of the West Indian pie, there would be fewer revolutions down there, and less room to charge the Negro with incapability of self Government."[18]

Throughout his career Rudd kept before his reading audience the concerns of African Americans, Catholics, women, and vulnerable people groups living beyond the borders of the United States. As a journalist he used his newspaper as a vehicle to faithfully raise a cry for justice wherever he saw the need. And his campaign for equality and justice would develop more fully as he sought to organize African American Catholics around the country for the purpose of addressing the needs of the black community both inside and outside the church.

CHAPTER EIGHT

Coming Together for Change

Daniel Rudd was an observant activist. He watched with interest as the various groups with whom he interacted organized to tackle matters unique to the constituencies of their respective organizations. He began contemplating the idea of bringing together African American Catholics for the purpose of addressing challenges being faced by the black community. The Congress of Lay Catholics, of which he was cofounder, seems to have been the fruit of his desire to bring lay black Catholics into common cause with laity from across all demographics represented in the American Catholic Church.

In the pages of the *ACT*, the editor enthusiastically endorsed the Afro-American League (subsequently the National Afro-American League) founded by well-known journalist and civil rights leader T. Thomas Fortune. Rudd viewed Fortune's effort as the latest incarnation of black community organization. According to Rudd, this history of collective action could be traced back to the establishment of the Colored Conventions movement in 1830. In support of Fortune's league Rudd wrote, "Let us organize and convince parties that we, like other races, are susceptible to the influences which go to make them respected in the community."[1]

Rudd also watched with interest the workings of the German Roman Catholic Central Verein, an organization of German-speaking societies charged with promoting the interests of German Catholics in the United States. In September of 1887 Rudd attended a gathering of this body in Chicago. He was subsequently called on to address the group. Upon returning from one such meeting, Rudd complained that though the Germans and Irish were organized, the same could not be said of African Americans.

Through the late spring and early summer of 1887, Rudd contemplated the merits of Catholic collective action. He proposed the idea of bringing together an English-speaking Catholic congress he hoped might be attended by all races. Rudd claimed that church leadership in England, Ireland, and the United States were all supportive of the idea. The proposed assembly bore some resemblance to the Congress of Lay Catholics that Rudd helped to organize in 1889.

Rudd was a strong believer in African American agency— the power of its community to address injustice both within the Catholic Church as well as in society more broadly. Before issuing the call for the congress, Rudd told his readers that those seeking freedom would necessarily be the ones who must first "strike a blow." Demonstrating a specific commitment to black Catholic agency, Rudd explained his decision to hold a conference. He believed the best way to win the black population to the Catholic Church was to "find out how many Catholics we would have to start with and then put that force to work."[2] After the congress was organized Rudd would continue to exult in the critical work being done by black Catholics.

In the months leading up to the call for the first congress, Rudd communicated his strong commitment to black Catholic activism: "The proposed Congress is intended to awaken the Negro Catholic to a sense of his duty. Important questions will be submitted and discussed. . . . We must work ourselves if we expect to accomplish anything. The Colored man is naturally religious. He believes; but 'Faith without good works will not save us,' say the doctors of the Church. Let us be up and doing."[3]

In May 1888 Rudd called on black Catholics from around the country to come together under the "blessing of Holy Mother, Church." The editor believed this group could serve as the "leaven" of the race lifting all African Americans both in the eyes of God as well as in the eyes of humanity. In this proposed gathering, delegates would become familiar with one another as they tackled challenges facing the black community. Despite the delicacy of the matter in the eyes of church leaders, Rudd emphasized the need to discuss questions affecting African Americans "irrespective of religion."[4] As Rudd contemplated the gathering of this assembly, he demonstrated a commitment to a Catholic reading of history. He claimed the Catholic Church had through history stood like a beacon pointing the way to a "higher and perfect civilization."[5]

Mindful of his white Catholic readers, Rudd also pushed them to live their egalitarian faith. He pleaded with Catholics to drop their racial bias because he believed such prejudice might "prevent the humblest of the creatures of Almighty God from coming into the fold." Rudd also raised a warning to individuals who would turn someone away from the church because of their bigoted words or actions. Finally, he offered something of a penance for those who might seek to make amends for past discriminatory behavior. They could take the hand of a non-Catholic member of the race and lead them into the Catholic fold.[6]

In June 1888 Rudd outlined what topics might be discussed in sessions of the congress. Adding to earlier and more innocuous proposals like becoming more familiar with one another and joining forces with clergy in order to win members of the race to Catholicism, Rudd emphasized the need to discuss improving the plight of African Americans. For Rudd "many grievances" blocked the path of progress. The editor pointed to the fact that black residents living in the North were barred from learning new trades, including working as blacksmiths, wheelwrights, carpenters, and bricklayers. As a result of racial prejudice, he contended that factory jobs were also out of the reach of many African Americans. Rudd further believed foreign mechanics and factory workers enjoyed an unfair advantage over similarly qualified black laborers. Finally, Rudd saw merit in sending a delegation from the congress to the upcoming convention of the Knights of Labor for the purpose of persuading the union to open its doors to black workers.[7]

The official call for the first Colored Catholic Congress was published in the *ACT* October 6, 1888. Parish organizations and societies were called on to elect delegates to the gathering. St. Augustine Parish, a leading black Catholic church located in the nation's capital, would host the meeting. In the planning stages, Rudd was pressed to win the support of key church leaders, some of whom worried over how far such an assembly might go in pushing its demands for equality. In order to win the approval of individuals like Fr. John R. Slattery, head of the American Josephites, and Cardinal James Gibbons, head of the American church, Rudd likely had to tamp down his hopes of addressing the injustices being faced by the nation's people of color. Noteworthy is the fact that in the call for the congress no mention was made of addressing racial discrimination. Instead Rudd stated the gathering would help bring black Catholics together to assess their strength and number in the service of aiding the clergy in the conversion and education of the race.[8]

Rudd and those who assembled to establish what has now become the National Black Catholic Congress were preaching a gospel aimed at meeting the real world challenges facing the black community. Many African American Catholics were not afforded the luxury of merely preparing themselves for the afterlife. In this respect, their approach resembled that of the promoters of the Social Gospel. Applying church teaching to society's inequities was a necessity. As the delegates pursued what might be termed a "justice ministry" approach, structural evils including the sin of racism came into clearer focus. These same sensitivities were not always evident in white church circles.

As the congress neared, Rudd found support among leaders of the American Catholic Church. A number of them even wrote letters of endorsement for the upcoming meeting. Bishop Alfred A. Curtis of Wilmington, Delaware, joined Archbishop Elder of Cincinnati in endorsing the meeting. John Slattery even forwarded twenty-five dollars to help underwrite the project. But perhaps the most important endorsement secured by Rudd was that of Cardinal James Gibbons.

Prior to the gathering of the first congress, Rudd was confronted with a dilemma—whether or not to allow women to be seated as delegates. The contentious issue appears to have caught the editor off guard. Though there was no clause in the call for the meeting that forbade women to serve in this capacity, the signers, he explained, felt it best for them to be represented by their male advisors. Whether this decision reflected Rudd's true sentiments on the matter or those of church leaders advising him is unclear. Lest Rudd be judged too harshly, it should be noted that women delegates were not seated at the Congress of Lay Catholics held eleven months later.

The First Colored Catholic Congress, January 1889, Washington, DC

A sense of excitement and expectation filled the room as delegates made their way into St. Augustine Church in Washington, DC, for the first meeting of the Colored Catholic Congress. It was New Year's Day, 1889. The final call for the congress, issued only days before the meeting, boasted sixty-nine signers. When the doors of the church opened, the crowd quickly filled all of the church's available seating. As others made their way into the full church, standing room was made in the aisles. By the time the service began, however, there was no room left in the building.

No doubt pride filled the hearts of the assembled delegates as Augustus Tolton, the nation's only openly recognized African American priest, celebrated High Mass. Tolton's priesthood itself stood in opposition to the thinking of those who believed persons of color to be intellectually and morally inferior to whites. His presence in the front of the assembly reinforced Rudd's claim that white Catholics were indeed open to the equality of the races.

The head of the American church, Cardinal James Gibbons, gave the opening sermon. His presence signified the extent to which Rudd had been able to motivate church leaders to give attention to the concerns of the black apostolate. The Catholic Church was a body that knew no "Jew or Greek, or Barbarian" Gibbons declared.[9] Jesus Christ, he contended, had effectively broken down the wall dividing men—making one family. He then pointed to the multiracial character of those offering Mass to the congregation. This, he said, was evidence of the church's commitment to making no racial distinctions between its members. But from the start, there were differences between what the white leadership thought the agenda should contain and what black delegates wished to take up. For his part, Gibbons recommended the agenda include Christian education, the merits of avoiding alcohol, and the practice of economy and industry among members of the race.

Despite the concerns of some white leaders, the delegates produced a final statement outlining the difficulties confronting African Americans. It called for the admittance of black workers into labor unions. The document also encouraged employers to hire black applicants. The church received some praise, particularly those religious orders that were working directly on behalf of African Americans. Finally, the statement bound delegates to the task of reaching the black community.

Following the success of the first congress, plans were made for a second. John M. Mackey, who was the pastor of St. Peter in Chains Cathedral in Cincinnati, agreed to host the gathering. By this time, the prelate had joined Rudd as associate editor of the *ACT*. His church appears to have been home to more African American families than any parish in the city. Mackey had taken special interest in working with African Americans. For example, he personally led a class on the sacraments. Some of the same material presented in the course appears to have been subsequently reproduced in the newspaper.

Congress of Lay Catholics, November 1889, Baltimore

Another important initiative promoted by Rudd was the Congress of Lay Catholics gathering that met November

11–12, 1889, in Baltimore. The *ACT* carried the announcement for the meeting in its November 2, 1889, issue. The gathering was to commemorate the centennial of the establishment of the Catholic hierarchy in the United States. Along with Henry J. Spaunhorst of St. Louis and William J. Onahan of Chicago, Rudd is listed as one of the three committee members charged with organizing the gathering. The fact that Rudd was listed at all must mean he played a central role. Internal evidence from the *ACT* suggests he may have approached the other planners with the idea for the congress.

When the congress opened on November 11, 1889, delegates from around the country represented the diversity existing in the Catholic Church. On this important anniversary, those present expressed their strong loyalty to the doctrines of the church and their allegiance to the country. Perhaps just as important to Rudd and African Americans in attendance was the manner in which people of color were received. The meeting provided yet another example of the church's Catholic spirit, one that stood in opposition to the spirit of Jim Crow. Rudd subsequently wrote, "Neither race, color nor section weighed a feather. Baltimore, which more than any of the other great southern cities clings to certain customs, did herself proud in honoring alike the three ethnic divisions of mankind so fully represented in the Congress. The Negro in his simple earnestness, the Caucasian in his Catholic solidity, and the Indian in his feathers were all received alike, socially and otherwise."[10]

Rudd viewed the gathering of the lay congress as the church at her best. It was a manifestation of a "deep feeling of Christian love and respect" that made wealthy Irishmen, Germans, and other Americans all "kneel at the feet of the Negro priest to ask him beg the blessings of Almighty God upon their devoted heads." This spirit of love and respect distinguished the church from other denominations that Rudd claimed would "send the Negro to heaven via a black ladder." Rudd challenged other race newspapers to publish his report. "We believe they will and from that reproduction will flow in strengthening tides a mighty stream of the race into the invincible and immortal Church of Christ our Lord."[11] In the end, the editor said of the gathering, "The Congress was a magnificent success in every way."[12]

Though Rudd was pleased with the congress, his satisfaction was not complete. A few weeks after the gathering, he had reason to complain that black newspapers were not reporting on the meeting. Had the "Negro Question" been ignored by the congress, Rudd reasoned, both the *New York Age* and the Detroit *Plaindealer* would have no doubt caused a "howl" that would have been "excruciating in its screeching." Rudd further commented, "Dear, dear contemporaries don't you know enough to know that 25 percent of all the Negros who profess any sort of christianity [sic] are going into the one true Church? Do you think that your dodging the real issue will hinder the magnificent growth of Catholicity? Once more we say that the teachings of the church through all the ages, is and has been the 'Fatherhood of God and Brotherhood of Man.' "[13]

The Second Colored Catholic Congress, July 1890, Cincinnati

The black Catholic community came together in the Queen City to attend the second Colored Catholic Congress. Varying estimates of the number of delegates in attendance were reported. One source claimed only 45 individuals were present, while another estimated 125. In Archbishop Elder's absence, Fr. Mackey of St. Peter in Chains Cathedral was called on to give the opening address. Though he did not directly mention Archbishop Ireland or his controversial sermon on the color line previously delivered at St. Augustine Parish in the nation's capital, it is clear Mackey wanted to stake out a more conservative stand on race relations— one markedly different from that of the archbishop.

From the very beginning of his sermon, Mackey voiced his disapproval of what he termed the "amalgamation" of the races. In opposition to Ireland's call to obliterate the color line, Mackey declared, "The individual of either race who disregards this line of demarcation drawn apparently by nature herself, is no credit to either race." Driving this same message home, Mackey expected the races to continue into the future on a separate, parallel trajectory, a course that would preclude any intimate comingling. In his mind, the precondition for the church's efforts on behalf of black citizens was an understanding that they would harbor no "need" or "desire" for "amalgamation with other races." With this imperative precondition established, the church would work to champion causes important to the black community. She would attempt to open the door to all trades and professions; she would advocate for the right of "well-conducted blacks" to sit at the table of gentlemen everywhere. Finally, she would welcome African Americans into the Catholic Church, including into her parish schools, benevolent societies, and confraternities.[14]

Rudd's *American Catholic Tribune* carried the words and inspiration of the congress to individuals unable to attend the gathering in person. Rudd recorded two moving speeches given on the second day of the Cincinnati meeting, one delivered by William S. Lofton, the second by Charles Butler. Lofton was a Howard-trained dentist from the Washington,

DC, area and an active member of St. Augustine Parish. In his address, he looked forward to a time when black Americans would "hail the dawn of the day when justice [would] hold the field a conqueror." He also offered praise for those allies in the church active in the promotion of the cause of justice. Not surprisingly, first on this list was Archbishop John Ireland of St. Paul.[15] Lofton's public recognition of Ireland could be interpreted as a not-so-veiled rebuff of the meeting's host, Fr. John Mackey, who opposed the removal of the color line.

Much of Lofton's speech was taken up with the importance of education. This pressing goal he placed only behind the need to know God. Lofton even challenged Mackey's more positive appraisal of the church's efforts on behalf of African Americans. He claimed the Catholic Church had given little attention to the issue of education for members of the black community. In his public criticism of members of the church hierarchy, which must have stung those present, Lofton declared, "We value our religion and Catholic training; we marvel that Divines of the church do not support their teaching by having Catholic colleges and schools open their doors to at least those of our Colored children who are well behaved and able to pay." Lofton also criticized the practice of forcing black Catholics into segregated seating. Here he quoted Ireland who had earlier stated, "No church is a worthy temple of God where a place is marked off for Colored people. It is a shame and scandal in the temple of God, when a man on account of his color is driven to an obscure corner or to a loft."[16]

Charles Butler's speech was likely just as odious to the ears of church leaders as Lofton's had been. Like Lofton he praised the work of Archbishop Ireland. Moreover, Butler, who served as a clerk in the US Treasury Department's Division of Appointments, drew attention to the large number of black church members being lost to the Catholic Church each year as a result of her failure to provide schools for the race. In Washington, DC, not one school was open to black students beyond the age of twelve, Butler told the gathered crowd. To begin to remedy this injustice, he proposed the establishment of a national vocational high school. Tellingly, neither Lofton's speech nor Butler's speech was mentioned in John Slattery's article about the congress subsequently published in *Donahoe's Magazine*. It might well be that the criticisms of the church raised by the delegates at Cincinnati were intentionally omitted because they served to cast the Catholic Church in a negative light.

The ongoing campaign for justice carried forward in the second congress by black Catholics, including Daniel Rudd, comes through in the inspiring final resolution. It merits a lengthy quotation:

> Proud therefore of our membership in Holy Church, and, as fully qualified citizens of the United States, standing ready at all times to obey the laws of our country as well as defend its flag if need be, with our lives, we feel that we are not asking too much in claiming the rights of simple but complete justice whether in Church or State.
>
> We ask more particularly of our Catholic brethren that the teachings of the Church, Who, in her expansive charity embraces, equally and to the fullest extent all the sons of Adam whether collectively or individually, be cheerfully and thoroughly practiced.
>
> This simple, straightforward, though respectful demand of ours, is but in keeping with the solemn declaration of the late General Congress of American Catholic laymen, who pledged themselves to do all in their power to ameliorate

the condition of the Colored race. Let Justice, therefore,
on the one hand, and charity on the other, be the double
watchword of all our brethren in their treatment of the
people of our race from the lakes to the gulf, from ocean
to ocean.[17]

More specifically, the document movingly implores Catholic
leaders to "see that no Catholic be deprived of a Catholic
education because of a foolish sentiment that has neither
place in Catholic life, nor foundation in Christian charity."
The resolution also called on all trade unions and labor
organizations to admit African Americans, while employers
from various sectors of the economy were urged to hire
black applicants "as help may be required, without discrimination and on the merit of their individual capacity, intel-
ligence and integrity."[18]

Another global justice concern taken up by the congress
and subsequently included in the meeting's final resolution
was a call to support Cardinal Lavigerie, archbishop of
Carthage and Algiers and primate of Africa, in his campaign
to halt the ongoing African slave trade. In the planning
stages for the second congress, Rudd had informed his readers of the need to take up this cause. The editor's understanding of the blight of the slave trade in Africa had been
expanded after he and his employee Robert Ruffin had met
with Lavigerie.

In the summer of 1889, Rudd and his agent in Boston
had made the trip to Lucerne, Switzerland, to attend a scheduled antislavery conference that was subsequently canceled.
Still the two met with the cardinal. The meeting obviously
made a deep impression on Rudd. The church leader kissed
both Rudd and Ruffin, charging them to work to eradicate
the practice of slavery in Africa. Rudd's concern over this

inhumane institution is evident from a subsequent editorial. The editor wrote, "Those who have not followed the public prints closely may not be aware of the fact that a million of people are captured annually in Africa, and either die of ill treatment or are sold into slavery. It is against this horrid traffic that the Church is directing her forces."[19] It is likely Rudd took a leading role in adding this antislavery plank to the congress's final statement.

The final resolution produced by delegates gathered in Cincinnati pledged support for the "Colored sisters" working to educate orphaned, black children. Not only did the document bind delegates to financially support the work of the black sisters, it also bound them to encourage vocations among young women of color. The resolution encouraged the practice of temperance in the black community. Members of the race were called on to join labor groups as well as Catholic charitable organizations. Finally, the document implicitly rejected a more circumscribed and restrictive understanding of equality. Instead the delegates enthusiastically endorsed the work of Archbishop Ireland. The document read, "While our entire country is still ringing from one end to the other with the noble and uncompromising words of that fearless and most sincere champion of the race, the Most Rev. Arch. Ireland, we tender to this great apostle of the North-west, the expression of our deep and lasting appreciation of his kind words in our behalf."[20]

The second gathering of the Colored Catholic Congress in Cincinnati gave a platform to many talented up-and-coming black Catholic activists. Those delegates playing an important role at the gathering included William S. Lofton, Charles Butler, D. S. Mahoney, John R. Rudd, Thomas W. Short, and S. F. Hardy. A number of these individuals were instrumental in the future work of the congress movement.

Following the Cincinnati meeting of the congress, Rudd took to his sick bed for several days. It is unclear what the nature of his ailment may have been. Yet working through articles and editorials written in the aftermath of the meeting, some disturbing clues come to the light. An article penned by Slattery claimed a number of delegates to the congress had severely criticized Rudd's newspaper, particularly its "make up, matter, and poor paper." Rudd's critic expressed his hope that the paper would be moved to Philadelphia and placed under the oversight of Fr. Patrick McDermott. Under this churchman's guidance Slattery believed the *ACT* might "become a source of incalculable good to the negro race."[21]

Rudd was obviously deeply bothered by the slight. Slattery had taken upon himself to publish his criticisms of the newspaper. It is unclear the extent to which such a perceived betrayal might have contributed to Rudd's debilitating "illness." But Rudd was indeed angered. In subsequent editorials he punched back with uncharacteristic candor. It was not his intention to please everybody, he remarked, and was grateful for the advice he received whether he chose to take it or not. As to the matter of moving the newspaper to Philadelphia, Rudd declared, "The American Catholic Tribune is well pleased with its present location. This paper is just where it will always be. No Change has ever been contemplated or mooted by us nor would any proposition to that effect be considered for a moment."[22]

It is difficult to reconcile Slattery's negative appraisal of the *ACT* with the praise this same publication had received in previous years. A number of influential church leaders unapologetically endorsed the newspaper. Delegates to the first meeting of the congress eighteen months earlier had also praised Rudd's publication. The *Journal*, a rival black Catholic paper that looks as if it were started in Philadelphia with Slattery's blessing, did not in any measurable way eclipse the quality of Rudd's newspaper. It is likely Slattery's criticisms of the *ACT* that had more to do with the fact that the church leader had no control over it or its content. It is also possible Slattery was put off because the newspaper competed with the two Josephite publications, the *Colored Harvest* and the *St. Joseph's Advocate.*[23]

The Third Colored Catholic Congress, January 1892, Philadelphia

Prior to the gathering of the third Colored Catholic Congress, which was set to meet in Philadelphia in January 1892, delegates including Rudd grew bolder in their promotion of a racial justice agenda. In December, only weeks before the scheduled opening of the congress, Rudd traveled to Washington, DC, to meet Lofton, who had been charged with publicizing the upcoming meeting. Upon his arrival Rudd learned Archbishop Ireland was scheduled to speak at St. Augustine Church. Rudd bemoaned the fact that he had not prepared to record the archbishop's sermon. At a meeting of the Knights of St. Augustine, Commandery No. 2, Ireland addressed the parishioners from the congregation. Upon the prelate's introduction, the crowd gave a five-minute ovation. In his comments to the group, Ireland encouraged the assembly to "proclaim" their "rights." He added, "Tell the Catholic world what you want, demand it, continue as you are and all shall be right."[24]

When the delegates arrived in Philadelphia a couple of weeks later, they were not met with the same type of encouragement the archbishop had previously urged on the group. A careful read of the *ACT* suggests a bit of anxiety among white leaders in Philadelphia. Any attempt on the part of the members of the congress to push for civil rights would risk their cause, the *Church News* reported. An effort to curtail the aspirations of the delegates was also echoed in Archbishop John Ryan's opening address. He called for moderation. Progress toward emancipation had come slowly, he explained, as had the elevation of African Americans to equality with other races. Political equality they had already won, the church leader contended. Other equalities would be worked out in "God's own time."[25]

If Rudd and the other delegates believed Ireland's push for the immediate recognition of the full equality of African Americans was on target, then Ryan's position must have evoked within them some measure of disappointment. But delegates to the meeting pressed forward undeterred. During their time in Philadelphia, they laid the groundwork necessary to form a permanent congressional organization. As in previous meetings, delegates called on the church to open to the black community the doors of educational opportunity. The diplomatic Rudd even took to the podium to condemn the practice of denying blacks admittance into Catholic secondary schools. Such discrimination, he explained, discouraged young black students and put their faith in jeopardy. These lost souls would subsequently leave the Catholic fold altogether, he warned.

Over the course of the meeting, a critique of the church's treatment of African Americans was raised. Delegate Robert N. Wood of New York proposed the formation of a committee to look into reports of discrimination against black Catholics. The decision to include the reading of a correspondence from Archbishop Ireland must have felt like salt in a wound to many of the nervous white Catholic leaders present and forced to listen. Ireland's letter expressed the need to open Catholic schools to black youth and said,

"Whenever there are not separate schools, fully equipped for the instruction of colored children, these are admitted on equal terms with the [white] children, into all public schools and surely it shall not be said that the State goes farther than the holy church in the application of the great Christian principles of the Brotherhood of Men and the common Fatherhood of God."[26]

Following the third congress a fissure seems to have divided black Catholic leaders. Rudd focused on the publication of the *ACT* and on his book detailing the first three congresses he helped to lead. In March 1893 *Three Catholic Afro-American Congresses* was published. At the same time in Philadelphia, leaders of a new, rival, black Catholic newspaper the *Journal* were distributing their first issues. Though Rudd graciously recognized the new publication, it appears the newspaper took much of the *ACT*'s market share and may have even contributed to the *ACT*'s demise. The friction between Rudd and the organizers of the third congress, whatever its nature, may have also led him to step back from taking a more active role in the fourth and fifth gatherings of the congress movement held in Chicago and Baltimore, respectively. Still Rudd appears to have endorsed the gatherings. Though Rudd moved to the sidelines following the third congress, he could take satisfaction in the emergence of a talented group of black Catholic leaders who took up his campaign for justice and courageously carried it forward.

CHAPTER NINE

Life after the *American Catholic Tribune*

In 1893 Rudd moved the struggling *ACT* to Detroit. The reason for the move is unclear. He may have hoped to revive his newspaper in a city where the collapse of another race weekly, the *Plaindealer*, had left something of a journalistic vacuum. But Rudd's best efforts were disappointed. By 1897 the *ACT* was no longer being published. Nor does Rudd's name appear in the city directory after 1898. His whereabouts from 1898 through 1910 has been a mystery scholars have yet to unravel.

Rudd's name appears in the US Census of 1910. By this time he was living in Bolivar County, Mississippi, in a community known today as Boyle. In the late nineteenth century the region was a frontier town offering the ambitious soul a means by which to earn a stake in the American dream. The enterprising Rudd likely was attracted to this part of the state because of the economic opportunity it offered to black laborers. During this phase of his life, the former editor revealed a genius to some extent hidden in his earlier work. In his mid-fifties at the time, Rudd worked as a lumber mill manager.

While working in Mississippi, Rudd became acquainted with Scott Bond, Arkansas's first black millionaire and an enthusiastic supporter of Booker T. Washington. Bond owned a number of farms in and around Madison, Arkansas, and needed someone to oversee his lumber operation. Rudd proved a good hire. He served the Bond family in a number of capacities. He managed the lumber operation and worked as an accountant; he subsequently supervised Bond's gravel business. While overseeing the gravel operation, Rudd even designed a loading machine. During this same period Bond signed a lucrative contract with the railroad company. One wonders if such a deal would have been possible without Rudd's innovative contribution. As a trusted advisor to Scott Bond, Rudd was asked to aid one of Bond's sons, Theophilus Bond, in the penning of Scott Bond's biography. In 1917 *From Slavery to Wealth: The Life of Scott Bond* was published. Though Rudd and Bond seemed to have enjoyed a cordial working relationship, the former subsequently left Madison to go to work with John Gammon, a black farmer of some means who lived near Marion, Arkansas.[1]

During Rudd's years in the South he maintained a relationship with the Catholic Church. Letters between Rudd and Bishop John B. Morris reveal the nature of their association. On one occasion Rudd asked the prelate for the privilege of representing the diocese at the black Catholic layman's convention that met in Washington, DC, in 1920. In reply Morris explained the diocese had less than five hundred black Catholics and so was not qualified to send a delegate. On another occasion Morris asked Rudd to represent black Catholics at the Arkansas Eucharistic Congress that was to be held in Chicago, but Rudd could not attend. Over time, the aging Rudd must have experienced seasons of disappointment as he watched Jim Crow become more ensconced across the nation. In the early decades of the twentieth century, it is difficult to find evidence to merit Rudd's faith in the church's commitment to equality and racial justice. Instead the church seems to have in many cases acquiesced to Jim Crow culture as did other Christian denominational groups.[2]

In 1932 Rudd suffered a stroke. He returned to Bardstown to convalesce. His condition did not improve, and on December 3, 1933, Rudd died. His seventy-nine years were not time enough for him to see the positive impact of his work.

Taking Up the Torch

Rudd's pursuit of justice yielded fruit long after he was laid to rest in Bardstown. His work was taken up by the Black Catholic Congress movement he had inspired. Further inspiration fueling justice-minded activists in the last decades of the twentieth century was a 1984 report issued by the nation's African American bishops entitled "What We Have Seen and Heard: A Pastoral Letter on Evangelization from the Black Bishops of the United States." In this watershed document one hears the echoes of Rudd's prophetic voice. As the editor of the *ACT* sought to bring Catholics together with the aim of improving their lot, the document also affirms the gifts African Americans have to bestow on the larger church, gifts rooted in the community's African heritage. The document also prioritizes evangelism. Rudd, with unflagging faith in the church, urged his black brothers and sisters to come into the fold. Here he believed they would

experience a faith family unpolluted by the racism so prevalent in Rudd's day. The editor's understanding of the rela-
tional quality of justice also comes through in the document.
Reconciliation can never simply be defined as "unilateral
elevation and another's subordination" but rather must be
constituted "where there is mutually perceived equality. . . .
This is what is what is meant by justice."[3] Justice so con-
ceived assumes a family community where no one group
enjoys privileges above another, but rather all live as children
of God, equal in his sight. This loving, egalitarian community
recalls Rudd's "new civilization." It paradoxically serves as
both the matrix out of which justice is birthed as well as the
full fruit of a thriving community.

Following the 1984 report, an effort to reestablish Rudd's
Colored Catholic Congress movement was initiated. As
scholars began researching Rudd, a new generation of
Catholic leaders saw in his life's work a courageous quest
for a faith-centered vision of justice. The National Black
Catholic Congress's website reflects some of the same pri-
orities Rudd championed in the *ACT*. Following their pa-
tron's lead, the organization has committed itself to the
evangelization of black Americans. This evangelization is
comprehensive and includes the improvement of the "spiritual, mental, and physical conditions of African Americans."
These commitments have been promoted with the goal of
achieving nothing short of the full freedom and growth of
African Americans, work that will not be completed until
all are recognized as full and equal participants in both society as well as in the church.

In 1987 under the leadership of Bishop John H. Ricard,
the Black Catholic Congress gathered in Washington, DC,
the sight of the first congress held nearly a century earlier.
Over fifteen hundred persons responded favorably to the

meeting's theme, "Here I Am Lord, Send Me," a focus drawn from the writings of the prophet Isaiah. In this first twentieth-century gathering of the congress, leaders hoped to build on the momentum stirred by the bishop's report "What We Have Seen and Heard." Members left the congress commissioned to carry forward a work of justice, a divine task inspired by the organization's trailblazing founder Daniel A. Rudd.

The National Black Catholic Congress movement now meets every five years taking up many of the same themes and challenges addressed in the first five nineteenth-century congresses. In 1992 members met in New Orleans for the seventh meeting of the congress. A focus of this gathering was the family life of African Americans. Here delegates passed a series of public policy and pastoral statements on issues ranging from welfare policy to the promotion of family life. The eighth congress was convened in Baltimore in 1997 under the theme "What We Have Seen and Heard: We Proclaim and Celebrate." As the title intimates, becoming a consistent witness for Christ was a primary point of concentration. A spirit of celebration attended the gathering. This jubilation was occasioned by the dedication of Our Mother of Africa Chapel at the National Shrine of the Immaculate Conception in the nation's capital.[4]

The ninth congress, held in Chicago in the fall of 2002, was the first of the congresses to be convened in the twenty-first century. Keeping with this milestone, the theme for the meeting was "Black Catholic Leadership in the 21st Century: Solidarity in Action." Plans were drafted to promote vibrant expressions of spirituality in parish life; affirm the presence and contributions of youth and young adults in churches; sustain Catholic education; advocate for social justice; eradicate racism; and strengthen bonds with Africa. Plans were also discussed to provide a compassionate response for those suffering from HIV and/or AIDS.[5]

The tenth gathering of the Black Catholic Congress was held in Buffalo, New York, in July of 2007, taking as its theme "Christ Is with Us: Celebrating the Gifts of the Sacraments." Some three thousand attended. The meaning of the sacraments of the church was emphasized. In this meeting the cancerous sin of racism was again addressed. A faith-based model for improving race relations was proposed in one important workshop led by Robert Ellis, Development Director for the Diocese of Grand Rapids, and Shelia Adams—Director of the Office for Black Catholics, Archdiocese of Chicago.[6]

The eleventh gathering of the congress was held in Indianapolis, Indiana, in July of 2012. This gathering was attended by twenty-five hundred participants from around the country. The working theme of the congress was "Faith, Engaged: Empower, Equip, Evangelize." The gatherers recognized the church as an "evolving" institution. It was becoming more ethnically diverse, more multilingual, more polycentric, more feminine, more collegial, and more concerned about charity and justice. Celebrating the rich heterogeneity of the church, the same statement went on to contend, the church in its diversity "reflects God's Trinitarian life."[7]

The meeting resulted in a commitment to develop a five-year pastoral plan. The plan was built on research that showed black Catholics have traditionally been highly engaged in their faith life. Conversely, leaders realized black Catholics were leaving the fold. The research supporting the plan of action determined that about 5 percent of the black population in the United States was Catholic. Outreach to youth was a topic addressed in the pastoral plan. Other areas of focus included parish registrations and closures, Catholic schools, marriage, spirituality, solidarity with immigrants, and the promotion of vocations among African Americans. Also getting some attention in the draft of the five-year platform was the need to promote the veneration of black saints. At the 2012 gathering attendees were encouraged to become more involved in pro-life issues as well as in the championing of the rights of the dispossessed and diverse people groups. Challenges including adequate housing, fair wages, family support, employment, and health care were a few of the topics covered under the umbrella of social justice concerns. Those familiar with the work of Rudd and other Colored Catholic Congress members from the nineteenth century know many of these same concerns were taken up as part of the platform of justice these visionaries promoted.

Concluding Thoughts

Many challenges threaten the church today as it attempts to model for the world a just equitable community. Perhaps the most pressing one is related to the polarization pitting communities against one another all across the country. People of color distrust those who serve in law enforcement; immigrants and citizens are at odds with one another in public discourse; the well-to-do are scapegoated as are society's most economically vulnerable.

Rudd believed the church to be a divinely ordered sanctuary—a space where fraternity and mutual love would necessarily characterize relationships. Convinced of the fundamental unity of the human family (the Fatherhood of God and Brotherhood of Man), Rudd urged the church to teach society respect. He hoped justice and equality would someday serve as the foundation of a "new civilization," one animated by love of God and love of neighbor.

Generations have passed since Rudd's death. The challenge is passed to all who are willing to be the people of

God in an often fractured and polarized world. May we indeed take up this grand work; may we be a community where respect is offered to the diverse other. As we carry this work forward, the echo of Rudd's prophetic message reaches our ears, encouraging us to press on in faith and calling us to live justly toward one another as the world looks on.

Notes

Introduction—pages 1–7

1. *The Christian Soldier*, quoted in "A Good Joke," *American Catholic Tribune*, May 17, 1890, 3.

2. This organization was also referred to as the "Colored Press Association" and the "Afro-American Press League."

3. See correspondence, W.J. Onahan to John R. Slattery, March 30, 1893; Slattery to W.J. Onahan, Easter Sunday (1893), both in Saint Joseph Society of the Sacred Heart Josephite Archives, Baltimore; Cyprian Davis, *The History of Black Catholics in the United States* (New York: Crossroads Publication Co., 1990), 182.

4. John H. Lamott, *History of the Archdiocese of Cincinnati, 1821–1921* (New York: Frederick Pustet Co., 1921).

Chapter One:
Enslaved in Catholic Kentucky—pages 9–15

1. Gilbert J. Garraghan, *The Jesuits of the Middle United States* (Chicago: Loyola University Press, 1983), 293.

2. Record of the Personal Property of Charles Haydon, Will Book, 9:494, Nelson County Court Records, Sutherland Building, Bardstown, KY.

3. C. Walker Gollar, "Catholic Slaves and Slaveholders in Kentucky," *Catholic Historical Review* 84, no. 1 (January 1998): 42–62.

4. Inventory and Appraisement of the Estate of Richard Rudd, Nelson County Court Records, Sutherland Building, Bardstown, KY.

5. Ibid.

6. Joseph H. Lackner, "Dan A. Rudd, Editor of the *American Catholic Tribune*: From Bardstown to Cincinnati," *Catholic Historical Review* 80, no. 2 (April 1994): 265.

7. Ibid.

8. "The Race Problem," *American Catholic Tribune*, April 29, 1893, 2.

9. *ACT*, November 18, 1887, 2.

10. *ACT*, June 3, 1887, 2.

11. Ibid.

12. Garraghan, *The Jesuits of the Middle United States*, 325–26.

13. Ibid., 330.

14. *ACT*, October 13, 1888, 2.

15. "Kamloops, B. C.," *ACT*, May 27, 1887, 1.

16. *ACT*, June 3, 1887, 2.

Chapter Two:
A Prophetic Voice in a Hope-Filled Season—
pages 16–27

1. "What Others Say of Us," *American Catholic Tribune*, June 17, 1887, 2; *ACT*, September 12, 1891, 2; M. Edmund Hussey, *1999 Sesquicentennial Directory St. Raphael Catholic Church* (Springfield, OH: St. Raphael Catholic Church, 1999), 8–11.

2. "Public Meeting of the Black Citizens of Springfield," *Springfield Republic*, April 13, 1882, 2; Lackner, "Dan A. Rudd," 268.

3. "Public Meeting," *Springfield Republic*, April 13, 1882, 2.

4. *ACT*, April 1, 1887, 2.

5. Armistead S. Pride and Clint C. Wilson, *A History of the Black Press* (Washington, DC: Howard University Press, 1997), 13.

6. *ACT*, August 12, 1887.

7. *ACT*, January 31, 1891, 2; "That Afro-American News Syndicate," *ACT*, November 14, 1891, 2.

8. Joseph H. Lackner, "The *American Catholic Tribune* and the Puzzle of Its Finances," *Records of the American Catholic Historical Society* (Spring/Summer 1995): 28–29; "Dissolution of Co-partnership," *ACT*, July 20, 1888, 3.

9. *ACT*, August 9, 1890, 2; *ACT*, June 8, 1889, 2.

10. *ACT*, August 9, 1890, 2; "Development of Africa," *ACT*, July 19, 1890, 2.

11. See for example, "Word of Approval," *ACT*, July 9, 1890, 2.

12. *ACT*, December 23, 1887, 2.

13. Joseph H. Lackner, "The *American Catholic Tribune*: No Other Like It," paper presented at the American Catholic Historical Association Meeting, University of Dayton, April 23, 2005, Dayton, OH, photocopy, 1–2.

14. Ibid., 4–5.

15. *ACT*, December 30, 1887, 2.

16. *ACT*, January 16, 1889, 2.

17. "Ratified in New York," *ACT*, March 2, 1889, 2.

18. "A South American Approval," *ACT*, July 22, 1887, 2; *ACT*, September 2, 1887, 2.

19. *ACT*, July 19, 1890, 2.

Chapter Three:
Finding Justice in the Catholic Church—
pages 28–35

1. *American Catholic Tribune*, November 5, 1892, 2.

2. *ACT*, March 9, 1888, 2.

3. "Our One Colored Parish," *ACT*, December 7, 1892, 2.

4. Ibid.

5. "Why the Afro-Americans Should Be Catholics," *ACT*, September 26, 1891, 2.

6. *ACT*, October 17, 1891, 2.

7. "Race Progress," *ACT*, March 16, 1888, 2.

8. *ACT*, December 16, 1887, 2.

9. *ACT*, February 2, 1889, 2.

Chapter Four:
Partners in Pursuit of Equality—pages 36–47

1. *American Catholic Tribune*, January 20, 1888, 2.

2. *ACT*, May 16, 1891, 2.

3. "C.K. of A.," *ACT*, 15 November 1890, 1; *ACT*, 15 November 1890, 2.

4. "C.K. of A.," *ACT*, 15 November 1890, 1; *ACT*, 15 November 1890, 2.

5. "Colored Catholics in St. Paul," *ACT*, April 19, 1890, 2.

6. Ibid.

7. Ibid.

8. "There is No Color Line," *Catholic Mirror*, May 10, 1890, 5.

9. Ibid.

10. "The Colored Problem," *Catholic Mirror*, May 10, 1890, 4; also quoted in "Archbishop Ireland and the Negro Press Comments," *ACT*, May 17, 1890, 2.

11. "Archbishop Ireland and the Negro Press Comments," *ACT*, May 17, 1890, 2.

12. *ACT*, January 24, 1891, 2.

13. *ACT*, May 10, 1890, 2.

14. "Archbishop Ireland and the Negro Press Comments," *ACT*, May 17, 1890, 2.

15. "A Brave Defense," *ACT*, May 24, 1890, 2.

16. "Archbishop Ireland and the Negro Press Comments," *ACT*, May 17, 1890, 2.

17. *ACT*, July 22, 1887, 2.

18. Patrick J. Ryan to Michael Augustine Corrigan, May 20, 1890, transcript in the hand of Patrick J. Ryan, Special Collections, Archdiocese of New York Archives, St. Joseph's Seminary, Yonkers, NY.

19. "The Congress Proceedings," *ACT*, July 19, 1890, 1.

20. Daniel Rudd, *Three Catholic Afro-American Congresses* (Cincinnati: *American Catholic Tribune*, 1893), 127.

Chapter Five:
A Foundation for Justice—pages 48–61

1. *American Catholic Tribune*, March 9, 1888, 2.

2. See Rabbi Edward N. Calisch, "A Case of Experience with The Negro Problem," *Reform Advocate*, quoted in *ACT*, March 5, 1892, 1; "The Same Old Story," *ACT*, March 5, 1892, 2.

3. *ACT*, July 6, 1888, 2.

4. "Quincy, Ill.," *ACT*, March 11, 1887, 4.

5. *ACT*, March 30, 1889, 2.
6. *ACT*, April 6, 1888, 2.
7. *ACT*, June 27, 1891, 2.
8. "The Same Old Satan," *ACT*, January 24, 1891, 2.
9. Ibid.
10. *ACT*, January 18, 1890, 2.
11. *ACT*, September 19, 1891, 2.
12. *ACT*, April 19, 1890, 2.
13. *ACT*, June 13, 1891, 2.
14. "Tis Done At Last," *ACT*, May 21, 1892, 2.
15. *ACT*, April 16, 1892, 2.
16. "Tis Done At Last," *ACT*, May 21, 1892, 2.
17. *ACT*, February 10, 1888, 2.
18. *ACT*, September 28, 1889, 2.
19. *ACT*, April 6, 1888, 2.

Chapter Six:
Campaigning for Equality and Racial Justice—
pages 62–74

1. Rayford W. Logan, *The Betrayal of the Negro from Rutherford B. Hayes to Woodrow Wilson* (New York: Collier, 1965), 161. Originally published as *The Negro in American Life and Thought: The Nadir, 1877–1901*. (New York: Dial Press, 1954).
2. *American Catholic Tribune*, May 31, 1890, 2.
3. *ACT*, November 30, 1890, 2.
4. *ACT*, October 25, 1890, 2.
5. *ACT*, April 13, 1888, 2.
6. Gary Dorrien, "Recovering the Black Social Gospel: The figures, conflicts and ideas that forged the 'New Abolition,' " *Harvard Divinity School Bulletin* 43, nos. 3–4 (Summer/Autumn 2015), accessed June 15, 2016, http://bulletin.hds.harvard.edu/articles/summerautumn2015/recovering-black-social-gospel.
7. "Lexington, Ky.," *ACT*, June 3, 1887, 2.
8. "Caucasians Must Rule," *ACT*, September 14, 1889, 2.
9. "Think! Consolidate! Agitate!," *ACT*, April 9, 1892, 2.

10. "Danger Ahead," *ACT*, May 14, 1892, 2.

11. *ACT*, August 5, 1887, 2.

12. Ibid.

13. *ACT*, April 25, 1891, 2.

14. *ACT*, September 13, 1890, 2; *ACT*, July 9, 1892, 2.

15. "Justice Reigns," *ACT*, October 19, 1889, 3.

16. *ACT*, June 10, 1887, 2.

Chapter Seven:
Matters of Justice for Catholics beyond Concerns of Race—pages 75–87

1. *American Catholic Tribune*, August 23, 1890, 2.

2. *ACT*, April 6, 1888, 2.

3. John T. McGreevy, *Catholicism and American Freedom* (New York: W. W. Norton & Company, 2003), 123.

4. "The National Press Association," *ACT*, August 12, 1887, 3.

5. *ACT*, November 21, 1891, 2.

6. *ACT*, October 7, 1887, 2.

7. "Ireland's Chances," *American Catholic Quarterly Review*, quoted in *ACT*, February 23, 1889, 2; *ACT*, June 25, 1892, 2.

8. "Pontiff and Pagan," *ACT*, November 17, 1888, 3.

9. *ACT*, June 6, 1891, 2.

10. Davis, *Black Catholics in the U. S.*, 118–21; 132.

11. James J. Kenneally, *The History of American Catholic Women* (New York: Crossroad, 1990), 13; Barbara Welter, "The Cult of True Womanhood, 1820–1860," *American Quarterly* 18, no. 2, pt. 1 (Summer 1966): 151–74.

12. Kenneally, 3–4.

13. James Cardinal Gibbons, *Our Christian Heritage* (Baltimore: John Murphy & Co., 1889), 361–71.

14. Ibid., 360–61.

15. *ACT*, July 22, 1887, 2.

16. "Woman's Suffrage," *ACT*, July 22, 1887, 1.

17. It is unclear the source of this estimation. Millions of slaves were imported to Brazil beginning in the mid-sixteenth century.

18. "The Same Old Story," *ACT*, May 23, 1891, 2.

Chapter Eight:
Coming Together for Change—pages 88–105

1. "The Afro American League," *American Catholic Tribune*, June 17, 1887, 2.

2. *ACT*, June 22, 1888, 2.

3. *ACT*, September 21, 1888, 2.

4. "Congress of Colored Catholics," *ACT*, May 4, 1888, 2.

5. *ACT*, May 18, 1888, 2

6. Ibid.

7. "The Proposed Congress of Colored Catholics. What Can It Do?," *ACT*, June 8, 1888, 2.

8. "A Call," *ACT*, October 13, 1888, 1.

9. See Gal 3:28.

10. *ACT*, November 16, 1889, 2.

11. Ibid.

12. Ibid.

13. *ACT*, November 30, 1889, 2.

14. "The Congress Proceedings," *ACT*, July 19, 1890, 1.

15. "The Congress," *ACT*, July 26, 1890, 1.

16. Ibid.

17. "Resolutions," *ACT*, August 30, 1890, 1.

18. Ibid.

19. Ibid.

20. Ibid.

21. John R. Slattery, "The Congress of Negro Catholics," *Donahoe's Magazine* 24 (1890): 269–71.

22. *ACT*, August 23, 1890, 2.

23. See Lackner, "The *American Catholic Tribune* and the Puzzle of Its Finances," 34.

24. "Washington, D.C.," *ACT*, December 19, 1891, 2.

25. *Church News* quoted in David Spalding, "The Negro Catholic Congresses, 1889–1894," *Catholic Historical Review* 55, no. 3 (October 1969); "The Third Congress," *ACT*, January 16, 1892, 1.

26. "The Third Congress," *ACT*, January 16, 1892, 3.

Chapter Nine:
Life after the *American Catholic Tribune*—
pages 106–13

1. Davis, *Black Catholics in the U.S.*, 213.

2. Davis, *Black Catholics in the U.S.*, 213–14.

3. "What We Have Seen and Heard: A Pastoral Letter on Evangelization from the Black Bishops of the United States," The Black Bishops of the United States, accessed August 30, 2016, http://www.usccb.org/issues-and-action/cultural-diversity/african-american/resources/upload/what-we-have-seen-and-heard.pdf.

4. John Rivera, "National Black Catholic Congress returns to Baltimore Convention was last here at end of 19th century," August 29, 1997, accessed July 10, 2016, http://articles.baltimoresun.com/1997-08-29/news/1997241066_1_catholic-congress-national-black-catholic-returns-to-baltimore.

5. Joseph N. Perry, "Black Catholic Congress IX and Future Directions," *New Theology Review* (May 2005): 25–35, accessed August 30, 2016, file:///C:/Users/Gary%20Agee/Downloads/358-1593-1-PB.pdf.

6. http://nbccongress.org/congress-x/pdfs/reflections-congress-x.pdf.

7. Zoe Ryan, "Black Catholic Congress develops five year plan," National Catholic Reporter, July 26, 2012, accessed July 15, 2016, https://www.ncronline.org/news/people/black-catholic-congress-develops-five-year-plan.

Bibliography

Primary Sources

American Theological Library Association, Chicago
American Catholic Tribune, 1887–1894. Microfilm.

Nelson County Court, Bardstown, KY
Commissioners Report of the Slaves of R. Rudd Appraisement & Allotments.
Inventory and Appraisement of the Estate of Richard Rudd.
Nelson County Deed Book, Vol. 21.
Record of the Personal Property of Charles Haydon. Will Book, Vol. 9, 494.

Saint Joseph Society of the Sacred Heart Josephite Archives,
Baltimore
William J. Onahan to John R. Slattery, March 30, 1893. Slattery Collection.
John R. Slattery to William J. Onahan, Easter Sunday, 1893. Slattery Collection.

Secondary Sources

Black Bishops of the United States. "What We Have Seen and Heard: A Pastoral Letter on Evangelization from the Black Bishops of the United States." Accessed August 30, 2016. http://www.usccb.org/issues-and-action/cultural-diversity/african-american/resources/upload/what-we-have-seen-and-heard.pdf.

Church News quoted in Spalding, David. "The Negro Catholic Congresses, 1889–1894." *Catholic Historical Review 55,* (1969): 346.

Davis, Cyprian. *The History of Black Catholics in the United States.* New York: Crossroads Publication Co., 1990.

Dorrien, Gary. "Recovering the Black Social Gospel: The figures, conflicts and ideas that forged the 'New Abolition.'" *Harvard Divinity School Bulletin* 43, nos. 3–4 (Summer/Autumn 2015). Accessed June 15, 2016. http://bulletin.hds.harvard.edu/articles/summerautumn2015/recovering-black-social-gospel.

Garraghan, Gilbert J. *The Jesuits of the Middle United States.* Vol. 2. New York: American Press, 1938. Reprint, Chicago: Loyola University Press, 1984.

Gibbons, Cardinal James. *Our Christian Heritage.* Baltimore: John Murphy & Co., 1889.

Gollar, Walker C. "Catholic Slaves and Slaveholders in Kentucky." *Catholic Historical Review* 84, no. 1 (January 1998): 42–62.

Hussey, Edmund M. *1999 Sesquicentennial Directory St. Raphael Catholic Church.* Springfield, OH: St. Raphael Catholic Church, 1999.

Kenneally, James J. *The History of American Catholic Women.* New York: Crossroad, 1990.

Lackner, Joseph H. "The *American Catholic Tribune*: No Other Like It." Paper presented at the American Catholic Historical Association meeting at the University of Dayton, April 23, 2005, Dayton, OH.

———. "The *American Catholic Tribune*: No Other Like It." *U.S. Catholic Historian* 25, no. 3 (Summer 2007): 1–24.

———. "The *American Catholic Tribune* and the Puzzle of Its Finances." *Records of the American Catholic Historical Society of Philadelphia* (Spring/Summer 1995): 25–38.

———. "Dan A. Rudd, Editor of the *American Catholic Tribune*: From Bardstown to Cincinnati." *Catholic Historical Review* 80, no. 2 (April 1994): 258–81.

——. "The Foundation of St. Ann's Parish, 1866-1870: The African American Experience in Cincinnati." *U. S. Catholic Historian* 14, no. 2 (Spring 1996): 13–36.

Lamott, John H. *History of the Archdiocese of Cincinnati, 1821–1921*. New York: Frederick Pustet Co., 1921.

Logan, Rayford W. *The Betrayal of the Negro from Rutherford B. Hayes to Woodrow Wilson*. Originally published as *The Negro in American Life and Thought: The Nadir, 1877–1901*. New York: Dial Press, 1954. Reprint, New York: Collier Books, 1965.

McGreevy, John T. *Catholicism and American Freedom*. New York: W. W. Norton & Company, 2003.

Perry, Joseph N. "Black Catholic Congress IX and Future Directions." *New Theology Review* (May 2005): 25–35. Accessed August 30, 2016. file:///C:/Users/Gary%20Agee/Downloads/358-1593-1-PB.pdf.

Pride, Armistead S., and Clint C. Wilson. *The History of the Black Press*. Washington, DC: Howard University Press, 1997.

Rivera, John. "National Black Catholic Congress returns to Baltimore Convention was last here at end of 19th century." August 29, 1997. Accessed July 10, 2016. http://articles.baltimoresun.com/1997-08-29/news/1997241066_1_catholic-congress-national-black-catholic-returns-to-baltimore.

Rudd, Daniel A. *Three Catholic Afro-American Congresses*. Cincinnati, OH: *American Catholic Tribune*, 1893. Reprint, New York: Arno Press, 1978.

Ryan, Zoe. "Black Catholic Congress develops five year plan." *National Catholic Reporter*, July 26, 2012. Accessed July 15, 2016. https://www.ncronline.org/news/people/black-catholic-congress-develops-five-year-plan.

Spalding, David. "The Negro Catholic Congresses, 1889–1894." *Catholic Historical Review* 55, no. 3 (October 1969): 346.

Welter, Barbara. "The Cult of True Womanhood, 1820–1860." *American Quarterly* 18, no. 2 (Summer 1966): 151–74.

Index